The Origins of the Russian Revolution
1861–1917

IN THE SAME SERIES

General Editors: Eric J. Evans and P.D. King

The Origins of the Russian Revolution 1861–1917

Second edition

Alan Wood

London and New York

I0770980

First edition published in 1987 by
Methuen & Co. Ltd

Second edition first published in 1993
by Routledge
11 New Fetter Lane, London EC4P 4EE

Simultaneously published in the USA and Canada
by Routledge
29 West 35th Street, New York, NY 10001

© 1987, 1993 Alan Wood

Typeset in 10/12pt Bembo by
Ponting–Green Publishing Services, Chesham, Bucks
Printed in Great Britain by
Clays Ltd, St Ives plc

Printed on acid free paper

British Library Cataloguing in Publication Data
A catalogue record for this book is available from the British Library

Library of Congress Cataloging in Publication Data
Wood, Alan
The Origins of the Russian Revolution 1861–1917/Alan Wood
p. cm. – (Lancaster pamphlets)
Includes bibliographical references
1. Russia–History–Nicholas II, 1894–1917.
2. Soviet Union–History–Revolution, 1917–1921–Causes.
I. Title. II. Series.
DK262.W67 1993
947.08'3–dc20 93–13451 CIP

ISBN 0–415–10232–4

Contents

Foreword

Lancaster Pamphlets offer concise and up-to-date accounts of major historical topics, primarily for the help of students preparing for Advanced Level examinations, though they should also be of value to those pursuing introductory courses in universities and other institutions of higher education. Without being all-embracing, their aims are to bring some of the central themes or problems confronting students and teachers into sharper focus than the textbook writer can hope to do; to provide the reader with some of the results of recent research which the textbook may not embody; and to stimulate thought about the whole interpretation of the topic under discussion.

Preface to the second edition

Since the first edition of this pamphlet was published in 1987, dramatic, and at that time unpredictable, changes have taken place in the former Soviet Union, a nation which was created by the revolutionary upheavals of 1917 and the Bolshevik victory in the ensuing Civil War (1918–22). In 1985, Mikhail Gorbachev became General Secretary of the Soviet Communist Party and inaugurated a programme of far-ranging economic and institutional restructuring (*perestroika*), and a policy of 'openness' and freedom of information (*glasnost*) unprecedented in Soviet experience. By 1991 his reforms had generated so much social discontent, political dissatisfaction, economic chaos and ethnic unrest in the non-Russian Republics, that in August of that year a cabal of 'hard line' politicians attempted to launch a *putsch* against him, placed him under house arrest, and declared a state of national emergency. The *putsch* was defeated, but in the whirlwind of political transformation that followed, the Communist Party of the Soviet Union was obliterated, Gorbachev was forced to resign, and the USSR was formally abolished. The Soviet period of Russian history was over.

This situation of revolutionary change and uncertainty, which is still going on inside present-day Russia, has had a profound impact on the way in which the history of the 1917 Revolutions is now understood, studied and taught in the country where it took place. Some of the new theories, circumstances and perspectives in the re-writing of the Russian Revolutions are discussed in a completely revised final chapter. Otherwise, the text remains substantially the same as in the first edition, and the interpretation of the forces which formed the origins of the Russian Revolution stays basically unaltered. The central thesis is still that the events of 1917 itself, to which a separate chapter is devoted, can only be properly understood against the complex background of social, political, economic and intellectual developments within the Russian Empire in the period which began with the emancipation of the serfs in 1861. The last decades of the nineteenth century were a period during which the peoples of the Russian Empire went through the painful and ambiguous process of what Marxist historians would describe as a transition from feudalism – characterized by autocracy and serfdom, to capitalism – marked in what was still a basically peasant country by an imperfect modern economic infrastructure, new urban-based social forces, and the tsarist government's reluctant experiments with quasi-parliamentary political and legislative institutions. It is in the volcanic soil of this transitionary era that the seeds of the Revolution were set.

A glance at the expanded and updated 'Suggestions for further reading' (pp. 56–8) will reveal that the authors of other recent treatments of the Russian Revolution, its background and its aftermath, have chosen rather different time-scales (e.g. 1900–1927, 1899–1919, 1917–1932) within which to set their analysis. The cut-off date of October 1917 in the present work is not intended to suggest that the revolutionary process stopped there. Obviously it did not, but the main emphasis remains on the *antecedents* of the February and October Revolutions, rather than their *consequences*, which, to some extent, have been dealt with in another pamphlet in this series.*

The transliteration, dating and nominative conventions used in the previous edition remain unchanged, as does the dedication. However, in addition to the original acknowledgements, I wish to express my thanks to those professional colleagues, both here and in the former Soviet Union, as well as to unknown readers, teachers and reviewers, who were kind enough to comment on the contents of the first edition. Where appropriate, their suggestions have been incorporated in the second.

Alan Wood
Lancaster, 1993

* Alan Wood, *Stalin and Stalinism*, Routledge, London, 1991

Notes and acknowledgements

All Russian forenames have been anglicized (thus Nicholas, rather than Nikolai). Surnames, placenames and Russian technical terms have been transliterated according to a common-sense, easily recognizable pattern which combines elements of the standard international systems.

Dates are given according to the Julian calendar which was used in Russia until 1918. In the nineteenth century this was twelve days, and in the twentieth century thirteen days, behind the Western (Gregorian) calendar.

Thanks are due to Eric Evans and David King for valuable editorial advice and to Brenda Wright for secretarial assistance; also to John Haywood for preparing the map on page xviii.

This pamphlet is dedicated to all former staff and students of Lancaster University's Department of Russian and Soviet Studies which, like the Russian Empire, though with less reason, is also a thing of the past.

Chronological table of events

Pre-1861

1584–1613	Period of social and political turmoil, the 'Time of Troubles'.
1613	Restoration of autocracy; Michael Romanov becomes tsar.
1613–96	Entrenchment of autocratic government; continuing civil, religious and military unrest.
1696–1725	Reign of Peter I (Peter the Great); Great Northern War (1700–21); Russia becomes a major European power.
1725–62	Era of 'palace revolutions'.
1762–96	Reign of Catherine II (Catherine the Great).
1773–5	The Pugachev rebellion.
1790	Publication of Radishchev's *A Journey from St Petersburg to Moscow*.
1801–25	Reign of Alexander I.
1825	Decembrist revolt.
1825–55	Reign of Nicholas I.
1836–48	'Westerner–Slavophil' controversy.
1848	Revolutions in Europe.
1853–6	Crimean War; Russia defeated.
1855–81	Reign of Alexander II.
1856	Alexander II announces intention to abolish serfdom.

1861	Emancipation of the serfs.
1861–4	Period of social and intellectual unrest; origins of revolutionary populism; first *Zemlya i volya*; 'era of manifestos'; Polish uprising (1863); trial and exile of Chernyshevsky.
1864	Introduction of local government and judicial reforms.
1866	Karakozov's attempt to assassinate Alexander II.
1866–74	'The White Terror'; further development of populist revolutionary theory.
1874	Military reforms.
1874 and 1875	The 'going to the people' movement.
1876	Formation of the second *Zemlya i volya*.
1879	*Zemlya i volya* splits over question of terror; formation of *Cherny peredel* and *Narodnaya volya*.
1881	Alexander II assassinated by *Narodnaya volya*.
1881–94	Reign of Alexander III.
1883	Formation in Geneva of first Russian Marxist group, the Group for the Liberation of Labour.
1893	Witte becomes Minister of Finance.
1894–1917	Reign of Nicholas II.
1894–1901	Programme of intensive industrialization.
1897–1900	Lenin in Siberian exile; perturbed by 'revisionist' tendencies in Social Democratic movement.
1898	First Congress of Russian Social Democratic Labour Party (RSDRP).
1900	First edition of *Iskra*; foundation of Socialist-Revolutionary Party (SRs).
1901–5	Economic slump; agrarian and industrial unrest.
1902	Publication of Lenin's *What is to be Done?*
1903	Second Congress of RSDRP; split between Mensheviks and Bolsheviks.

1904–5	Russo-Japanese War; Russia defeated.
1905	Revolutionary turmoil throughout Russia following 'Bloody Sunday' massacre (January); tsar promises a constitution (August); general strike, formation of St Petersburg Soviet, imperial manifesto authorizing elections to State Duma (October); suppression of Moscow rising (December).
1906	First State Duma; Stolypin becomes Prime Minister.
1906–11	Stolypin's agrarian reforms.
1907	Second State Duma; Stolypin alters electoral laws.
1907–12	Third State Duma.
1911	Stolypin assassinated.
1912	Lena goldfield massacre; renewed industrial unrest; split between Mensheviks and Bolsheviks becomes final.
1912–17	Fourth State Duma.
1912–16	Rasputin scandal; widening rift between government and society.
1914	Germany declares war on Russia.
1915	Nicholas II becomes C-in-C; relations between government and Duma deteriorate; formation of Progressive Bloc.
1916	Murder of Rasputin.

1917

Jan.–Feb.	Strikes and civil unrest in Petrograd.
26–27 Feb.	Troops refuse to fire on demonstrators; garrison 'joins' the revolutionary movement.
27 Feb.	Formation of Petrograd Soviet of Workers' Deputies.
1 March	Order No. 1 of Petrograd Soviet drafted; election of soldiers' committees called for.
2 March	Nicholas II abdicates; formation of first Provisional Government; inauguration of 'dual power'; programme of democratic reform and civil liberties announced.

3 April	Lenin returns to Russia; formulates *April Theses*; calls for 'All Power to the Soviets'.
20 April–2 May	Protest against Milyukov's 'war note'; collapse of first Provisional Government.
5 May	Formation of second Provisional (coalition) Government; socialist ministers appointed; Kerensky becomes Minister for War.
3 June	First All-Russian Congress of Workers' and Soldiers' Deputies opens.
18 June	Launch of the Galician offensive.
2 July	Trotsky joins Bolsheviks.
3–4 July	Violent anti-government demonstrations in Petrograd.
5–7 July	Arrest of Bolshevik leaders ordered; Lenin goes into hiding.
8 July	Kerensky becomes Prime Minister.
16 July	Kornilov appointed C-in-C.
23 July	Trotsky arrested.
July–Sept.	Agrarian disturbances, working-class militancy and army desertions on the increase.
27–30 Aug.	Re-arming of Red Guards; Kornilov's attempted military coup defeated.
September	Trotsky freed; becomes chairman of Petrograd Soviet; Petrograd and Moscow Soviets obtain Bolshevik majorities; Lenin revives slogan 'All Power to the Soviets'.
10 Oct.	Lenin attends meeting of Bolshevik Central Committee; his call for armed insurrection approved.
20 Oct.	First meeting of Military Revolutionary Committee of Petrograd Soviet.
24–25 Oct.	Armed workers and soldiers, led by Bolsheviks and organized by Military Revolutionary Committee, take over key buildings and installations in Petrograd.
25–26 Oct.	Provisional Government ministers arrested; Bolshevik coup announced at second Congress of Soviets; Menshevik and SR delegates withdraw in protest.

26–27 Oct.   Congress of Soviets adopts Decree on Peace and Decree on Land; appoints first Soviet government, the all-Bolshevik Council of People's Commissars, with Lenin as chairman.

Glossary of Russian technical terms

Bolshevik	'majority-ite': member of Lenin's 'hard line' faction of the Russian Social Democratic Labour Party
bunt	spontaneous peasant uprising; riot
Cherny peredel (pronounced 'chorny')	Black Repartition: populist revolutionary party opposed to use of political terror
dvoevlastie	dual power: used especially of the sharing of political power between the Provisional Government and the Petrograd Soviet, March–October 1917
dvoryanstvo	land-owning (and before 1861 serf-owning) nobility
Duma	Assembly or Council: especially the State Duma, an elected quasi-parliamentary institution, 1906–17
intelligentsia	radical intellectuals
Iskra	'The Spark': Marxist revolutionary newspaper founded by Lenin in 1900
Izvestiya	'News': newspaper of the St Petersburg and Petrograd Soviet
Kadet	member of the moderate Constitutional Democratic Party (from the Russian initials K–D)
khlyst	literally, 'a whip'; member of self-flagellating religious sect to which Rasputin belonged

khozhdenie v narod	'going to the people': mass crusade of young populists to the peasantry, 1874 and 1875
kulak	literally, 'a fist'; derogatory term denoting, imprecisely, a rich peasant
Menshevik	'minority-ite'; member of the moderate, anti-Bolshevik faction of the Russian Social Democratic Labour Party
Molodaya Rossiya	'Young Russia'; inflammatory revolutionary manifesto circulated in 1862
narod	the people: in nineteenth-century usage, usually referring to the peasantry
Narodnaya volya	The People's Will: revolutionary terrorist organization responsible for the assassination of tsar Alexander II
narodnichestvo	Populism: a body of social and political ideas and organizations claiming to represent the communal interests of the peasantry
narodnik (pl. *narodniki*)	a populist: member of the populist movement
obshchina	Russian peasant commune or community
Pravda	'Truth': Bolshevik party newspaper, founded 1912
pogrom	violent attack on racial or social minority group; especially those directed against Jews
pud	unit of weight: 36.1 lbs or 16.38 kilograms
soviet	council: especially the Soviet of Workers' Deputies established first in 1905 and again in 1917
Sovnarkom	acronym for Council of People's Commissars: revolutionary government of Bolsheviks, set up in October 1917
Trudovik (pl. *Trudoviki*)	member of the Labour Group, a liberal–left coalition in the State Duma
Zemlya i volya	Land and Liberty: revolutionary populist organization, 1861–4 and 1876–9
zemstvo (pl. *zemstva*)	organ of rural local government, established in 1864

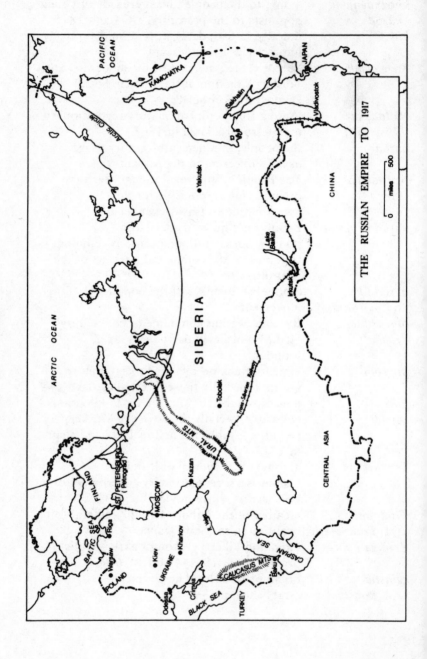

THE RUSSIAN EMPIRE TO 1917

PACIFIC OCEAN

KAMCHATKA

Arctic Circle

ARCTIC OCEAN

JAPAN

Sakhalin

Vladivostok

CHINA

0   miles   500

Yakutsk

SIBERIA

Lake Baikal

Irkutsk

Trans-Siberian Railway

URAL MTS.

Tobolsk

CENTRAL ASIA

ST. PETERSBURG (Petrograd)

FINLAND

BALTIC SEA

Riga

MOSCOW

Kazan

Volga

CASPIAN SEA

Warsaw

POLAND

Kiev

Kharkov

UKRAINE

CAUCASUS MTS.

Baku

Odessa

Crimea

BLACK SEA

TURKEY

1
Introduction

The Russian Revolution of 1917 is arguably the most important event in the political history of the twentieth century. A contemporary observer of the Revolution, the American journalist John Reed, entitled his famous account of those events *Ten Days That Shook the World*, and the tremors and reverberations of the upheaval still continue to be registered today. Seventy-six years after the event (at the time of writing) the shock-waves emanating from Russia in 1917 still have a direct or indirect impact on a whole range of political, economic, ideological, diplomatic, and military problems throughout the world. An appreciation of the causes, course and consequences of the Russian Revolution is not, therefore, merely a matter of historical interest, but something which is crucial to a proper and informed understanding of the political world in which we live, and in which the former Soviet Union – a state and society born of that Revolution – has played such a crucial role.

This pamphlet confines itself to an examination of the causes and course of the Revolution, from the emancipation of the Russian peasant serfs in 1861 to the Bolshevik seizure of political power and the establishment of the first Soviet government in October 1917. Why begin an examination of the 1917 Revolution in the year 1861? It is not necessary to subscribe to the Marxist–Leninist view of history to agree with Lenin's own opinion that the origins of the Revolution can be traced back to the unsatisfactory legislation which abolished serfdom in Russia in 1861. The ambiguous and internally contradictory programme of administrative reform which followed the Act of Emancipation generated new social, political and intellectual forces which were, however, confined within the rigid political framework of an absolutist, autocratic state. It is a physical, if not a historical, law that an uncontrolled steamhead of pressure building up inside an inflexible container with no room for expansion, no structural elasticity and no in-built safety-valves will inevitably explode and shatter the vessel. Those dangerous pressures and forces, both latent and active, were there for everybody to see and feel in the decades preceding 1917. Both for the autocracy and for the opposition, revolution was always a real possibility. Russian intellectuals constantly wrote and talked about it; activists organized for it; the government legislated against it; and the combined forces of the military and the police were constantly on the alert to suppress it. But it was the masses, the Russian people, who eventually made it. What follows seeks to describe and analyse some of the objective circumstances and subjective factors which contributed to that process, and which created those tensions and contradictions within the Russian Empire which proved ultimately unsusceptible of any other than a revolutionary solution. First, though, it is necessary to identify some of the salient characteristics of the tsarist regime and to trace the earlier traditions of revolutionary opposition to it.

2

Autocracy and opposition

The imperial regime: contrasts and contradictions

The Russian Empire at the time of the Revolution was a land of glaring contrasts. It was the largest land-empire in the world. From the heart of eastern Europe to the Pacific coast, and from the Arctic Ocean to the deserts of Central Asia and the Chinese borders, it sprawled – like the Soviet Union after it – over an area which covers roughly one-sixth of the earth's total land surface. A mismatch of territories and population, however, meant that whereas more than two-thirds of the country lay east of the Ural mountains in the vast, frozen expanses of Siberia, the bulk of the population resided and worked in the European provinces of Russia, Ukraine, Byelorussia, Poland (which was then an integral part of the Empire) and the Caucasus. The first Russian ruler to style himself Emperor (as distinct from tsar) was Peter I (Peter the Great, r. 1696–1725). The realm which he inherited from his seventeenth-century Muscovite forebears was already of considerable dimensions across the Eurasian land-mass, but it was his most enduring achievement to establish Russia's presence as the dominant power in northern and eastern Europe as a result of his victory over Sweden in the Great Northern War (1700–21).

The significance of Russia's entry into Europe cannot be exaggerated. Equally portentous were the reciprocal effects of

Europe's impact on Russia. The main thrust of Peter's reforms was to reshape the military and civilian administration of his country based on European models and to force the members of his landowning service nobility (*dvoryanstvo*) to adopt western-style habits, manners, education and attitudes. In this way Peter created a great division in Russian society – or, rather, he created two societies. On the one hand was the educated, westernized *dvoryanstvo*, which in the half-century after Peter's death became transformed into a fully fledged, leisured, land- and serf-owning nobility enjoying most, if not all, of the privileges of a European aristocracy. On the other hand were the Russian people (*narod*), the enserfed peasants, who continued to be ruthlessly exploited, fleeced and conscripted, while at the same time remaining sunk in a vast swamp of ignorance, misery, superstition and periodic famine. This social and intellectual chasm separating the nobility from the *narod* was a manifestation of the complex and ambivalent nature of the relationship between 'modern' Europe and 'backward' Russia which was a major *leitmotif* of the country's history throughout the nineteenth century.

Further examples of ambiguity and contradiction may be found in the political structure, economic relationships, military power and even the cultural achievements of Russia on the eve of revolution.

In the first place, the Russian emperor was an absolute autocrat. That is to say, there were no legal or constitutional constraints on his or her exercise of political power, choice of government ministers and officials, or formulation of national policies. A word from the tsar was sufficient to alter, override or abolish any existing legislation or institution. During the eighteenth and nineteenth centuries, several attempts had been made to draw up proposals for some kind of constitutional reform which would limit the tsar's powers, but none of them was successful. It was not until the revolutionary disturbances of 1905 that the last Russian tsar, Nicholas II (r. 1894–1917), was forced to authorize the holding of elections for a consultative and legislative national assembly known as the Imperial State Duma. However, despite the tsar's reluctant concession to the principle of some kind of limited participatory politics, the legalization of political parties, and the promulgation of a set of Fundamental Laws, the form of government still remained an

4

absolute autocracy. In other words, if the autocrat wished to abolish the constitution (and the Duma with it), then the constitution invested him with the authority to do precisely that. Neither fish nor fowl, the notion of a 'constitutional autocracy' was not only impractical, it was clearly a political absurdity which was doomed to failure.

In economic terms the situation was similarly problematic. Russia's industrial backwardness in comparison with the other major European powers had been exposed and highlighted by its defeat in the Crimean War (1853–6). Consequently, although not immediately, the government embarked on an intensive programme of industrialization at the turn of the century which catapulted Russia from being one of the least economically developed countries in Europe to one of the world's leading industrial producers. In the process Russia rapidly took on all the appearance and substance of a modern capitalist economy. For the first time in its history the country developed a large industrial labour force, or proletariat, and an economically powerful middle class of businessmen, bankers, lawyers, financiers, and factory-owners. At the same time, however, the great majority of the population, about 80 per cent, was still made up of communally organized peasants, working and living in their villages in conditions which had altered little since the eighteenth century. Even many town dwellers were officially registered as peasants, and Russia was still an overwhelmingly agrarian society. This existence of a modern, industrial society cheek-by-jowl with a large, land-hungry peasantry whose economic interests were long neglected by the government is a key factor in an understanding of the nature of the 1917 Revolution.

Also vital to an understanding of the events of that year is the role of the military. And here, too, we are faced with another apparent paradox. The power and prestige of the Russian Empire ultimately rested on the strength of its armed forces. The Russian army was the largest military force in the world, and was utilized not only for fighting foreign wars but also for maintaining internal order and suppressing civilian disturbances which threatened the stability of the regime. In the wake of Russia's defeat in the Crimea, there followed a series of radical military reforms in the 1870s which sought to reorganize and re-equip her forces for the tasks of modern warfare. Despite these changes, however, an overestimation of her strength resulted in further military disaster, this time at the hands of the Japanese in the war of 1904–5. The mighty Russian Empire was defeated by a relatively tiny Asiatic country which had, however, modernized itself more successfully and efficiently than its enormous, and apparently more powerful neighbour. The omens for Russia's involvement in the First World War were therefore hardly auspicious. Whether her disastrous performance in that conflict precipitated the Revolution of 1917 or not is a question that will be discussed in a later section, but the paradox is clear: on the one hand a great imperial power still with formidable military resources at its disposal, and on the other an army that seemed increasingly incapable of fulfilling its tasks, either of waging victorious war or of containing the internecine forces of civil unrest.

Culturally and intellectually, too, Russia during the reign of Nicholas II was a country which presented two different faces to the world. The two decades or so before 1917 have been described as the 'Silver Age' of Russian culture, the 'Russian Renaissance', and similar expressions which emphasize the innovative nature and high aesthetic quality of its artistic and literary achievements. Indeed, many of Russia's poets, painters and musicians formed the avant-garde of contemporary European culture. The plays and short stories of Anton Chekhov and Maxim Gorky, the poetry of Alexander Blok and the symbolist school, the music of Scriabin, Stravinsky and Prokofiev, new dramatic techniques pioneered by Stanislavsky and Meyerhold and the philosophical–religious ideas of Berdyaev and Rozanov, as well as the scientific discoveries of such scholars as Mendeleyev and Pavlov, were all of them characteristic of this age of intense cultural activity and attainment. The achievements are undeniable, but they were of course the exclusive preserve of the educated upper classes and intellectual élite. By contemporary western standards, levels of popular education and literacy in Russia were distressingly low. The majority of the peasant population was still illiterate, and in any case had far more urgent problems of sheer day-to-day survival to struggle with. There was little lyricism, learning or beauty in the life of the masses, and to many it seemed that the elegant outpourings of the intelligentsia were a self-indulgent abnegation of social and moral responsibility before the Russian people. Once again we are faced with a contradiction: that of a country whose brilliant artistic, scientific and literary achievements were in the forefront of European civilization, but the majority of whose population could not read or write its own language.

A further complicating factor in considering the state of the Russian Empire on the eve of revolution is the ethnic composition of the population. Out of a population in 1917 of 163 million, Russians accounted for only 40 per cent of the total. The rest was composed of a huge heterogeneous and multilingual collection of national minorities of widely differing size and levels of civilization. Throughout the history of the Empire these had periodically expressed their discontent at their subject status and at continuing Russian domination. This manifested itself in many forms from acts of individual protest and civil disobedience to full-scale and fully-armed national insurrections calling for separation and autonomy. These were always mercilessly suppressed. The Polish uprisings of 1830 and 1863, for instance, were followed by executions and the exile of tens of thousands of Polish patriots to permanent exile in Siberia. Among the other nationalities, the Jews in particular suffered from a variety of restrictions on their residence, education, professional opportunities and economic activities. They were, too, the regular victims of officially connived-at campaigns of mob violence, arson, looting, and rape – the notorious *pogroms*. Apart from Poland and the 'Jewish pale', anti-Russian feelings ran high elsewhere in the Empire, and among the centrifugal forces impelling the tsarist regime towards its final collapse, the movements for national independence among the non-Russian peoples were an emotionally charged and extremely potent factor.

The Russian Empire at the beginning of the twentieth century, therefore, contained a highly volatile mixture of ostentatious wealth and grinding poverty; power and debility; backwardness and modernity; despotism and urgent demand for change. Examples were everywhere to be found of juxtaposed barbarism and sophistication; European and Asiatic traditions; advanced technology and primitive techniques; enlightenment and ignorance. This is of course not a situation which is historically peculiar to Russia, and is indeed to be found in many underdeveloped or developing societies throughout the world today. However, the stark contrasts and contradictions existing in

Russia in the inter-revolutionary period between 1905 and 1917 led the great Russian writer, Leo Tolstoy, to remark ironically that Russia was 'the only country in the world where Chengiz-Khan enjoys the use of the telephone'.

The revolutionary tradition

The Romanov dynasty which was destroyed by the Revolution of 1917 was itself born of a quarter-century of revolutionary turmoil which racked Russia at the turn of the sixteenth century, a period traditionally known as the 'Time of Troubles' (1584–1613). The appointment of Michael Romanov as the new tsar in 1613, while solving the immediate political problem, did not offer any easy solution to the country's continuing social and economic difficulties, and the mid-seventeenth century was marked by so many instances of riot, mutiny, rebellion and religious schism that the Russian historian Klyuchevsky called this period the 'Time of Revolt'. From its very inauguration, therefore, the new regime was threatened with a series of potentially revolutionary challenges to its authority which set the pattern for the next three centuries of autocracy and opposition.

Most of these early disorders were elemental, savage, anarchical and not directed towards any specific political purpose. In particular, they were not directed against the tsar or, more precisely, against the autocracy as an institution. Indeed, it was a feature of many popular movements in the seventeenth and eighteenth centuries that they were headed by a pretender to the throne, an imposter claiming to be the rightful tsar who would restore the people's rights and redress their grievances. Peter the Great's reign of terror provoked much popular resistance which, on the whole, he managed to contain, though only with a battery of brutal reprisals. His failure to nominate an heir before his death in 1725 inaugurated a period of political confusion which is sometimes referred to as the 'Era of Palace Revolutions'. However, the rapid turnover of unremarkable characters occupying the Russian throne between 1725 and 1762 had absolutely no revolutionary implications for the structure of the Russian state or society. It was merely a matter of exchanging one monarch for another, purely as the figurehead for this or that particular court faction, clique or favourite. One thing these 'palace revolutions' did demonstrate, however, was the importance of maintaining the loyalty of the senior military, in particular the palace guards regiments, who often acted in the role of 'kingmakers'. This eighteenth-century tradition of the regimental coup and the crucial part played by the military élite at times of political crisis will be returned to at a later stage.

One of the most significant of the palace conspiracies was that of 1762 which resulted in the installation as Empress of Catherine II (Catherine the Great). It was during her long reign (1762–96) that two portentous events took place, each representing a major strand in the fabric of the revolutionary movement as it developed over the next century and a half. The first of these was the massive Cossack and peasant revolt led by the pretender Emelyan Pugachev between 1773 and 1775. In its geographical extent, in its numerical support, in the scope of its popular appeal and the wide range of its adherents – Cossacks, religious schismatics, factory-workers, native tribesmen and peasants – the Pugachev rebellion represented the most dangerous threat to the stability of the Russian state since the Time of Troubles. In the event the revolt was crushed, its leader's tortured body publicly butchered, and a bloodthirsty campaign of executions and reprisals carried out in the affected regions. Pugachev was dead, but his ghost continued to haunt the autocracy, and the spirit of his rebellion to inspire those later revolutionary activists who believed in the innately antiauthoritarian and insurrectionary nature of the Russian *narod*.

If Pugachev was the personification of popular revolt, then the case of Alexander Radishchev (1749–1802) epitomizes the phenomenon of theoretical criticism and radical intellectual challenge to the regime which was to grow in such menacing proportions during the course of the nineteenth century. In 1790 Radishchev published a trenchant criticism of Catherine's Russia in the guise of a travel-diary entitled *A Journey from St Petersburg to Moscow*. Its appearance – with its bitter indictment of serfdom, militarism, corruption and tyrannical government and its advocacy of legality, human rights and individual liberty – was a literary and political bombshell. Radishchev was arrested, interrogated and banished to Siberian exile. This turned out to be the opening shot in a long-drawn-out battle between the Russian government and members of the critical – later militant, and eventually revolutionary – intelligentsia. As long as the popular forces represented by Pugachev, and the intellectual challenges represented by Radishchev remained isolated from each other, as by and large they did during the following century, then the regime was relatively secure. When, however, in the early twentieth century the intelligentsia and the *narod* joined forces, like two dangerous chemicals, the resultant explosion swept away the tsarist social and political order of which they were both a product.

The first open attempt at revolutionary change which combined intellectual opposition with the familiar techniques of the military coup – but as yet eschewed popular participation – was the ill-fated and abortive Decembrist revolt of 1825 (so called after the date of the insurrection on 14 December). The unexpected death of Alexander I (r. 1801–25) precipitated the plans of a group of highly educated, but middle-ranking, army officers to stage a military *putsch* which would overthrow the autocracy and introduce some kind of constitutional monarchy or even a republican form of government. The rebellion was easily suppressed; five of its leaders were hanged and over a hundred other officers sentenced to exile in Siberia. The major reason why the attempted revolution did not succeed was that there was *no revolutionary situation*. When the Decembrists decided to take to the streets there was no national emergency – merely a minor hiccup over the royal succession. There was no economic crisis, no external threat, no breakdown in the social order, no mass disturbance – in fact none of the objective circumstances which usually constitute the prerequisite for successful revolution, as was the case in 1917. But although it failed – perhaps *because* it failed – the Decembrist revolt can properly be regarded as the beginning of the nineteenth-century revolutionary movement. Its members were revered as martyrs, and the ideals and example of these 'gentry-revolutionaries' continued to inspire later generations of reformers, radicals and revolutionaries alike.

The reign of the new tsar, Nicholas I (r. 1825–55), has been described as 'the apogee of absolutism'. But despite the reactionary, militaristic and obscurantist nature of his rule, some remarkably vigorous intellectual activity did take place during his reign, one of the most significant manifestations of which was the so-called 'Westerner–Slavophil' debate of the 1840s. Put very simply, the Westerners were those intellectuals who believed that the answer to Russia's problems lay in following

10

the example of European civilization. In particular they admired the western traditions of constitutional government, respect for the rights of the individual, rational philosophy, and the rule of law. Some of the more radical Westerners were also influenced by contemporary French socialist thinkers and by the theories of the German philosopher, Hegel, which one prominent Westerner described as the 'algebra of revolution'. Instinctively rebelling against the harshness of contemporary reality in Russia, and reinforced by these theories, the radical Westerners of the 1840s began to think in terms of revolution as providing the only means of changing that reality for the better.

The Slavophils on the other hand declared that what was wrong with the Russia of Nicholas I was already too much Europeanization, too much bureaucracy and officialdom, and a breakdown in what they believed to be the traditional harmoniousness of Russian society. Taking as the starting point of their philosophy the traditions and teachings of the Russian Orthodox Church, the Slavophils thought that Russia's future greatness lay in a return to the imagined virtues of her Muscovite past. They talked about the decadence and 'rottenness' of modern European civilization and contrasted it with the unspoilt, Orthodox Christian qualities of the Russian peasant. Above all, they pointed to the collective organization of the traditional peasant commune (the *obshchina*) as proof of the inherent moral and social superiority of the Russian people over the individualism, competitiveness and socially divisive egocentricity of Europeans.

It is hard to exaggerate the impact of Westerner–Slavophil controversy on the future intellectual, and even political, history of Russia. Many of the later disputes and divisions within the Russian intelligentsia, between different factions, schools of thought and political parties can be analysed in terms of those who sought what they believed to be a rational, logical and universal solution to Russia's problems and those who professed to be more alive to the idiosyncrasies of Russia's own peculiar cultural and social traditions. Indeed, both the dichotomy and the debate are still detectable in the political confrontations within Russia in the last decade of the twentieth century.

3
Reform and reaction

Emancipation and administrative reform, 1861–81

The emancipation of the serfs has been variously described as the 'most important single act of legislation in the entire history of Russia', and as being 'not worth the paper it was written on'. The arguments over the reasons for the government's decision to undertake this enterprise need not detain us here. What is important are the conditions and consequences of the settlement. It is, however, worth noting briefly that Alexander II (r. 1855–81) did not abolish serfdom out of any altruistic desire for an improvement in the lot of the Russian *narod*. Fear, rather than philanthropy, forced him to embark on a process which, following the Crimean débâcle, was seen to be essential to the economic and political survival of the Empire. The memory of Pugachev's hordes cannot have been far from Alexander's mind when he declared in 1856 that, if serfdom *was* to be abolished, 'it is better that it should be abolished from above, rather than wait until it abolishes itself from below'.

The essential features of the complex legislation were as follows. First, the serfs were given their technical, legal liberty, that is they were no longer the private property of their masters and were free to trade, marry, litigate and acquire property. Second, after a period of 'temporary obligation' during which they continued to perform some of the duties pertaining to their former serf-status, they were to begin paying a series of 're-demption payments' to the government for the land-allotments which had been assigned to them from their previous owner's estate. The high level of the redemption dues, set at 6 per cent interest over a period of forty-nine years, meant that the peasants were forced to pay a price for their land which was far in excess of its current market value, and represented a 'hidden' compensation to the *dvoryanstvo* for the loss of their servile labour.

Another crucial feature of the legislation was the fact that, although freed, the peasants were still organized within, and legally bound to, their village commune or *obshchina*. Both the freedom and the land which they received were granted not on an individual but on a collective basis. The commune wielded extensive powers over its members, both of an economic and of a quasi-judicial nature. Taxes, redemption payments and other dues were communally collected and paid; in areas where land was periodically redistributed among the peasants rather than held in hereditary tenure, the *obshchina* was responsible for the reallocation of land-allotments among the individual house-holds in the commune; no peasant was free to leave the commune without the permission of the village elders; and the commune was empowered to banish its wayward members to exile in Siberia. Peasants were still subject to corporal punish-ment, military conscription, payment of the poll-tax and certain other obligations from which other social classes were exempt. In other words the peasantry did not enjoy equal status with the other classes in Russian society. It was more of a separate 'caste', with its own internal structures, procedures, laws and economic arrangements. Moreover, the retention of the *obsh-china* as an official institution, although firmly rooted in Russian tradition, meant that in effect the peasant had merely exchanged bondage to the serf-owner for bondage to the commune. Lack of capital investment, periodic reallocation of land, primitive agricultural methods, crippling financial burdens and impedi-ments to mobility ensured that the agrarian sector of the Russian economy more or less stagnated for the next forty years. In terms of popular protest, too, the countryside remained remarkably quiescent during this period, though the obvious inequities and economic hardships imposed by the emanci-pation statutes were later to be dramatically highlighted by recrudescence of mass peasant disturbances at the start of the new century.

Following the abolition of the serf-owners' seigneurial rights over their former bondsmen, the government was logically faced with the necessity of constructing some new form of local government organization and judicial procedures to replace the old feudal institutions which existed under serfdom. Accordingly, legislation was drafted which, commencing in 1864, established new organs of local government in the countryside called rural councils, or *zemstva*. These were set up at both district and provincial levels, and comprised three 'elements': elected councillors; the permanent, paid officials or civil servants of the *zemstva*; and the professional employees of the councils such as schoolteachers, doctors, lawyers, agronomists, and other technical experts who actually carried out the day-to-day work in those areas of public welfare for which the *zemstva* had responsibility. Major administrative and financial restrictions meant, however, that the work of the *zemstva* and urban equivalents, the town councils, were seriously impeded and undermined. The *zemstva* were also very limited in their geographical extent and at the time of the 1917 Revolution functioned in only forty-three of the seventy provinces of the Russian Empire. The electoral system, too, left much to be desired. Suffrage was based on property qualifications which were pitched so high as to ensure that an overwhelming preponderance of the *zemstva*'s membership was drawn from the landowning nobility and the very wealthy urban classes. Despite some peasant representation on the *zemstva*, local affairs were still, after emancipation, very much in the hands of the local nobility, though these were now increasingly tied by bureaucratic and financial constraints imposed from the capital. Notwithstanding these drawbacks, the *zemstva* were remarkably successful in promoting welfare and public services in those areas where they existed. They also provided a forum in which members of society could gain some experience of participatory politics, albeit at local level, and also an opportunity for the intelligentsia, through its professional activities as the 'third element' of the *zemstva*, both to serve and to gain first-hand experience of the life of the Russian *narod*.

The administration of justice in Russia before the emancipation of the serfs was notoriously inefficient, long-winded,

14

corrupt and socially discriminatory. In 1864 a new judicial system was introduced which for the first time in Russia strove to incorporate some of the west-European concepts and principles of 'the rule of law': trial by jury; equality before the law; irremovability and proper training of judges; the establishment of a professional bar; public reporting of trials; and the separation of the judiciary from the legislature and executive. As in the case of the *zemstva*, the new judicial system was a distinct advance on the inequitable and labyrinthine procedures which it replaced. Similarly, however, it was not without its imperfections. Among the most glaring was the retention of the local peasants' courts which were still empowered to mete out corporal punishments. Also, the police still enjoyed extensive powers of arrest and punishment without trial of persons considered to be socially or politically undesirable. In times of social unrest martial law was regularly imposed; this overrode the civil courts and allowed the use of corporal and even capital punishment in the suppression of popular disorder. Furthermore, Russia's long tradition of arbitrary rule and illegality meant that notions of modern jurisprudence were very slow in penetrating both the official and the popular consciousness. Nevertheless, however flawed, the reformed judicial system did go a long way to meet standards of impartial justice, and the courts provided both a forum and another opportunity for the public voicing of non-conformist and critical opinion. Many members of the newly established legal profession later played a prominent part in anti-government politics and acted as a buffer between the people and the state.

The local government and judicial reforms were the most important (the emancipation apart) of a whole series of administrative and institutional changes which affected most areas of Russian life during this period. Reforms in the secondary and higher educational system, relaxation of censorship regulations, new developments in finance, trade and communications, and a thorough overhaul of the organization, training, recruiting and equipment of the Russian army were all symptomatic of the transition that Russia was slowly undergoing from a semi-feudal to something approaching a modern capitalist society. The paradoxical consequences of that process have been discussed above. Alongside the new institutions, remnants of the old regime still survived – most obviously of course the autocracy

– and the reforming tsar resolutely refused to listen to those progressive-minded members of the nobility who urged him to 'crown his reforms with a constitution'. The period of 'Great Reforms' was also an era of rising, though frustrated, expectations, and in the teeth of the government's refusal to alter the political structure of tsarism, and against the disappointment of the emancipation settlement, more and more members of the radical intelligentsia were becoming attracted by the prospect of popular revolution as the only means by which the Russian people might gain real 'land and liberty'. These two words – land and liberty (*zemlya i volya*) – later became the slogan and the rallying-cry of the Russian revolutionary populist movement which was to form the major focus of opposition to the policies of the 'Tsar-Liberator'.

Revolutionary Populism, 1861–81

Revolutionary Populism – or *narodnichestvo* – is the word used to describe both the theories and practical activities of Russia's militant intelligentsia in the 1860s and 1870s who attempted to bring about fundamental social and political change to the country in what they perceived to be the interests of the Russian *narod*. If necessary this was to be achieved by violent revolution. Whatever their individual or group differences – and there were many – the populists (*narodniki*) all shared a common vision of the destruction of the tsarist social and political order and its replacement by an agrarian–socialist society based on the collectivist traditions and institution of the Russian peasant commune. All insisted, too, that a purely Russian path of social and economic development must be trodden which would avoid the pitfalls and horrors of western capitalism. The *obshchina*, they believed, was a guarantee that this could be achieved. The *narodniki* were not opposed to industrialization as such. What they argued was that the communal principles of the peasant *obshchina* and the workers' co-operative should be retained and translated into the organization of trade and industry without subjecting Russia to the evils of exploitation, proletarianization and pauperization which were features of the capitalist mode of production.

The father of Russian Populism was Alexander Herzen

(1812–70). Disillusioned with European bourgeois civilization after witnessing the failure of the 1848 revolutions, this radical Westerner began increasingly to draw inspiration from some of the Slavophils' views, and to see the peasant commune, with its traditions of collectivism, mutual responsibility and redistribution of land, as the embryo of a future socialist society in Russia. His ideas were still amorphous and subject to frequent modification, but his amalgam of western socialism and Russian peasant collectivism certainly represents the first stage in the history of Russian Populism. The next stage was dominated by a man of altogether different character, Nicholas Chernyshevsky (1828–89). A man of more plebeian origins than the aristocratic Herzen, Chernyshevsky became the main spokesman and ideologue of the new post-Crimean generation of the intelligentsia, composed of young men and women who were more hard-headed, materialistic, impatient, uncompromising and, ultimately, revolutionary in their outlook than the 'men of the forties'. In his own writings he brought to bear a more solid, scholarly and dispassionate approach than Herzen to the major economic, social and political issues of the day. Owing nothing to the Slavophils' idealized vision of the *obshchina*, and basing his views on firmer historical and economic grounds, Chernyshevsky nevertheless argued that the retention, even the rejuvenation, of the commune was the best guarantee of a more equitable future for the Russian people. Nor was he seduced into thinking anything good would come out of the negotiations for the emancipation of the serfs. An article which appeared in 1859, clearly reflecting Chernyshevsky's intellectual position at the time, urged its readers not to be taken in by Alexander II's apparently good intentions, and proposed that the answer to the people's problems lay literally in the people's own hands: 'Only the peasants' axes can save us. Nothing apart from these axes is of any use . . . Summon Russia to arms!'

It was, however, only in the years immediately after the emancipation that any form of practical revolutionary activity took place. The immediate reaction of the liberated serfs was a mixture of bewilderment, anger and dismay which expressed itself in a number of disturbances throughout the country. These were swiftly and brutally suppressed. After the initial outrage, however, it is remarkable how quickly the countryside settled down and, seemingly, came to terms, albeit grudgingly, with the

17

new arrangements. The intelligentsia, too, began to voice its discontent. The first revolutionary organization since the Decembrists – calling itself *Zemlya i volya* ('Land and Liberty') – came into being, though its composition, membership, aims and objectives still remain unclear and it soon petered out with no concrete achievements. At the same time, the appearance and circulation of a number of political broadsheets and propaganda documents of a more or less inflammatory nature have led some observers to call these years the 'era of manifestos'. One of them in particular is worthy of comment. It was entitled *Molodaya Rossiya*, 'Young Russia', and was written by a 19-year-old student, Peter Zaichnevsky (1842–96). Despite the violent tone of its rather adolescent rhetoric, *Molodaya Rossiya* did set out a coherent programme of social and political objectives together with a rather gory scenario for revolutionary action which envisaged the slaughter of the entire 'Imperial party'. It also clearly identified the problem of the relationship between the revolutionary intelligentsia and the *narod*, a problem which Zaichnevsky tackled by proclaiming that the revolutionary masses must be led by a disciplined, centralized party organization which would, moreover, establish a post-revolutionary dictatorship to supervise the introduction of the new social and political institutions. Among these, Zaichnevsky's insistence on the paramount role of the *obshchina* places him squarely in the populist tradition, but his advocacy of an élite leadership for the revolution makes his manifesto one of the first voicings of that tendency in Russian political thought usually referred to as 'Jacobinism': that is, the belief that a popular rising must be organized and led by a centralized, revolutionary vanguard. This subject will be returned to below.

The bloody suppression of the Polish national uprising in 1863, the disappearance of *Zemlya i volya*, the return of relative calm to the countryside, and the arrest, trial and exile of Chernyshevsky in 1864 marked the end of the immediate post-emancipation unrest. In 1866 things took a different turn. Dmitry Karakozov (1840–66), a member of a tiny, clandestine revolutionary cell in Moscow, decided that the fundamental cause of the people's misery was the autocratic state – which in popular language meant the tsar. He therefore took it on himself to assassinate Alexander, and attempted to carry out his intention on 4 April 1866. His shot went wide, and Karakozov was arrested and later hanged. Other members of his organization were exiled to Siberia, and there set in a period of intense police repression which is sometimes referred to as the 'White Terror'. In order to escape arrest and possible exile after the Karakozov affair, many members of the radical intelligentsia fled abroad to Switzerland where they continued their studies and where, between 1866 and 1874, the ideology of Russian Populism developed along divergent lines. The three major tendencies were associated with the theories of Peter Lavrov (1823–1900), Michael Bakunin (1824–76) and Peter Tkachev (1844–86).

Lavrov believed that it was the task of the intelligentsia to engage itself in a programme of education, preparation and propaganda which would gradually raise the level of its own, and the people's, political consciousness to the point where they, the people, would rise, overthrow the state and establish a socialist society. In his *Historical Letters* he spoke of the moral debt of the 'penitent gentry' to the Russian *narod*, and of the need to redeem their debt by putting themselves at the service of the people – but only when they and the people were fully ready. Bakunin, on the other hand, believed passionately that there was nothing that the intelligentsia could teach the *narod*. 'The Russian people', he said in a famous phrase, 'is revolutionary by instinct and socialist by nature.' Invoking the spirit of Pugachev, Bakunin scorned the idea that it was the intelligentsia's task to indoctrinate the people. On the contrary, he put his faith in the spontaneous peasant insurrection – the *bunt*. If the intelligentsia had any role at all, it was simply that of helping the peasants to co-ordinate their separate rebellions into a nation-wide revolution that would destroy the tsarist state and leave the people to organize themselves into a federation of autonomous, self-governing communes. 'We must not act as schoolmaster for the people,' he said, 'but we must lead them to revolt.' Leading the people to revolt was also a central feature of Tkachev's philosophy. Unlike the anti-authoritarian, anarchist Bakunin, however, Tkachev produced the most fully-articulated expression of that 'Jacobin' Populism which appeared in Zaichnevsky's manifesto. Tkachev impatiently exhorted the intelligentsia to organize itself for revolutionary action and to lead the masses in both the destruction of the old order and the construction of the new. Some authors have argued that Tkachev's emphasis on discipline, leadership and organization foreshadows some of

19

Lenin's views on party organization and the relationship between the revolutionary party and the proletariat – a topic discussed in the following chapter.

In the 'mad summer' of 1874 an amazing phenomenon occurred. Without leadership, without organization and without planning, thousands of young intellectuals, both men and women, left their homes, universities and employment and joined in a mass, spontaneous movement, almost a crusade, to spread the socialist gospel throughout the Russian countryside. This was the famous 'going to the people' (*khozhdenie v narod*). There was no immediate signal for the movement. It represented a curious mixture of semi-digested socialist theories (both Lavrovist and Bakuninist), genuine sympathy for the sufferings of the peasantry and youthful enthusiasm to serve a noble cause, and was marked by an almost missionary commitment and zeal. The whole affair was a miserable fiasco. Many became disillusioned with the sullen, conservative and unresponsive nature of the peasants themselves; others were struck down by diseases endemic in the Russian countryside; some were arrested by the local police; and many were actually detained by the suspicious peasants and handed over to the authorities for 'speaking against God and the tsar'. Hundreds were imprisoned and later put on public trial in St Petersburg and Moscow. The intelligentsia had 'gone to the people'; the people had sent them back. Nothing could more clearly or tragically illustrate the continuing gulf that separated Russia's educated classes from the *narod*.

The failure of the 'movement to the people' actually to move the people forced the revolutionaries to reappraise the situation. They now reverted to the techniques of organization, conspiratorial planning and underground activities aimed at the 'disorganization' of the state. In 1876 a second *Zemlya i volya* party was founded. Its programme was impeccably populist in its orientation, but more and more its leading members began to concentrate on the immediate political tactics and to lose sight of the broader strategy of preparing for mass social revolution. The crisis within *Zemlya i volya* came to a head over the specific question of terror. A policy of armed resistance to arrest and consequent shoot-outs with police and prison authorities had escalated into pre-emptive assassination attempts on government and police officials. Faced with the growing wave of terrorist violence, the government imposed a state of emergency and martial law, and the vicious circle of assassination, executions, revenge and reprisals intensified. Finally, in 1879, the party split into two factions. One, called *Cherny peredel* ('Black Repartition'), opposed the use of political violence as being counter-productive, a betrayal of populist principles, and not conducive to the ultimate aims of the revolution. The other, *Narodnaya volya* ('The People's Will'), dedicated itself to a continuation of the terror campaign, arguing that this would enfeeble the state and hasten the onset of a revolutionary situation. On 26 August 1879 the Executive Committee of the *Narodnaya volya* solemnly condemned Alexander II to death, and after several unsuccessful attempts the Tsar-Liberator was finally blown to pieces on 1 March 1881 by a terrorist bomb. Five leaders of the conspiracy were arrested, tried and publicly hanged. The rest of the radical intelligentsia was decimated by imprisonment, exile and emigration.

It would be a mistake to regard the execution of the regicides and the ensuing collapse of *Narodnaya volya* as the end of revolutionary Populism in Russia. The subsequent government reaction and the growing preoccupation of more and more radical intellectuals with the revolutionary theories of Karl Marx (1818–83) did not mean that the populist tradition died out. Marx's revolutionary philosophy was based on a study of the industrial history and political economy of the advanced capitalist societies of western Europe, and many still continued to believe that his class-based ideas of 'bourgeois-democratic' and 'proletarian-socialist' revolution were inapplicable to backward, agrarian, autocratic Russia. How the early Russian Marxists coped with the theoretical and practical implications of this situation is dealt with in a later section. The assassination of Alexander II in 1881 and the foundation of the first Russian Marxist group in 1883 did not therefore mark the end and the beginning of two separate chapters in the history of the revolutionary movement. Russian Populism and Russian Marxism were, as one writer has put it, 'two skeins entangled'. Despite the eventual political triumph of the Marxist Bolshevik party in 1917, the populist tradition with its belief in the value of the commune, the socialization of the land, and the need for a non-capitalist road of development was to remain a powerful and – from the government's point of view – dangerous force on the Russian political scene until, and beyond, 1917.

21

Not surprisingly, the reaction of the incoming tsar to the politically futile assassination of his father was harsh. Alexander III (r. 1881–94) was by nature bigoted, authoritarian, fiercely chauvinistic, suspicious of intellectuals, and also anti-Semitic. The grey eminence behind the throne was the Procurator of the Holy Synod (the government minister responsible for church affairs), Constantine Pobedonostev (1827–1907), a man who combined extreme erudition with a hatred bordering on paranoia of anything which detracted from the principles of autocratic government, Orthodox Christianity and Russian nationalism. He dismissed those who continued to talk about a constitutional form of government in Russia as 'half-wits and perverted apes', and his fanatic religiosity and intolerance of change set their stamp on the entire reign, a period sometimes referred to as the 'era of petty deeds'.

The first casualty of the new regime was the misnamed Loris-Melikov 'Constitution'. Shortly before his death Alexander II had authorized his Minister of the Interior, Count Loris-Melikov (1825–88), to prepare a project which, had he survived, *might* have led to the summoning of a national consultative assembly to deliberate and advise on the preparation of legislation. Hardly the draft of a constitution, it was nevertheless immediately scrapped by the new emperor who described it as a 'criminal document'. Loris-Melikov was dismissed. In a drive to purge the country of subversive and 'untrustworthy' elements, the next Interior Minister granted the police extensive new powers of surveillance, arrest and administrative (i.e. extra-judicial) exile. Originally a temporary device, the Statute on Measures to Preserve National Order and Public Peace (14 August 1881) was systematically renewed every three years till 1917, and so sweeping were its powers that Russia was effectively turned into a police state. Lenin once described the draconian legislation as 'the *de facto* constitution of Russia'.

Apart from abandoning Loris-Melikov's plan and augmenting the arbitrary powers of the police, Alexander III's government sought in other ways to reverse, or at least weaken, the effects of his predecessor's reforms. More and more criminal cases were removed from the jurisdiction of the new courts as recourse was increasingly made to administrative procedures and special tribunals in which cases were often heard in camera. Likewise, the *zemstva* were made the subject of new legislation which drastically curtailed their already limited areas of competence and independence. Most importantly, the establishment in 1889 of a new corps of centrally appointed government officials with wide-ranging administrative powers over the *zemstva*'s activities more or less removed what little authority they had. This did not represent, as is sometimes alleged, the restoration of the land-owners' rights over the peasantry so much as a reinforcement of the central government's authority over the local and regional communities as a whole.

It is hardly surprising that the regime's suspicion of local and regional initiatives should have extended to the non-Russian peoples and non-Orthodox religions of the Empire. Jews, Polish Catholics, Baltic Protestants, central-Asian Muslims and Russian sectarians all fell victim in a greater or lesser degree to the obnoxious and ill-conceived policies of 'Russification'. A whole battery of discriminatory legislation was aimed at eradicating various manifestations of non-Russian national identity and un-Orthodox religious practices. Even the use of native languages – for example Polish in Polish schools – was selectively banned and the learning of Russian made compulsory in some of the non-Russian borderlands. As mentioned previously, the Jewish community was singled out for particularly vindictive treatment and racialist attacks which eventually led to the emergence of a 'Zionist' movement in search of a separate Jewish homeland.

Artistically and intellectually, the reign of Alexander III was not distinguished by any especially remarkable achievements and indeed the government brought in stricter censorship controls, muzzled the press and caused the closure of many journals. In schools and universities the reintroduction of the hierarchical principle ensured that proper educational opportunities were denied to the lower classes of society. This policy was purpose-fully designed – in the words of a notorious government memorandum – to prevent the children of 'coachmen, servants, cooks, washerwomen, small shopkeepers and other similar persons' from acquiring ideas above their station which might lead them to question the 'natural and inevitable inequality in social and economic relationships'.

If the overall atmosphere of the 1880s was one of stagnation, mediocrity and repression, there is one area in which some modest progress was made which paved the way for the more spectacular achievements of the following decade – and that is in the development of industry. Although the emancipation settlement had not generated either the capital or the labour necessary for a major programme of industrialization, nevertheless certain important developments did take place between 1861 and 1894 which laid down the infrastructure for what was to become Russia's industrial revolution. The establishment of banks, joint-stock companies and other financial institutions, increasing factory and urban growth, and greater labour mobility were matched by steady industrial progress. Output of iron, steel, coal and oil rose significantly, and railway construction expanded from 1,500 kilometres of track in 1861 to 30,500 in 1890. Likewise the industrial labour force more than doubled between 1860 and 1890 to about one and a half million. Most of this expansion was the result of private enterprise – particularly in railway construction. The appointment, however, of Sergei Witte (1849–1915) as Minister of Finance in 1893 marked a crucial turning point in the industrial development of Russia.

Although many elements of the so-called 'Witte system' were in place before 1893, it was Witte whose enthusiasm forced through a programme of rapid industrial expansion which had not only economic, but also profound social and political consequences. The distinguishing features of the 'system' were as follows: the leading role taken by the government in planning and finance; emphasis on capital goods rather than consumer goods industries; investment fundraising by increased taxation of the already over-burdened peasantry; and encouragement of massive investment of foreign capital – particularly French, Belgian and British. Central to the programme was the remarkable expansion in railway construction – the most spectacular project being the laying of the 7,000 kilometre Trans-Siberian Railway linking the rail networks of European Russia with the Pacific coast. The enormous demands of the Trans-Siberian on the metallurgical and coal industries played an important role in the whole industrialization process, and its completion around 1901, with the consequent fall-off of government orders, contributed much to the economic slump which followed Witte's 'boom'. The following figures for output in key sectors of industry between 1890 and 1900 illustrate the scale of the upsurge: coal rose from 367 million *puds* (1 *pud* = 16.38 kilograms) to 995, iron ore from 106 to 367, and petroleum from 241 to 632 million. Between 1887 and 1897 the value of textile production rose from 463 million to 946 million rubles. This rapid growth rate was characterized by high concentration of production in key geographical regions – St Petersburg, Moscow, Ukraine, the Baku oilfields and the Urals – and high concentration of workers in very large-scale industrial enterprises. In 1900 almost half the industrial labour force was located in factories which employed more than 1,000 workers – very high by contemporary European standards. Most commentators agree that living and working conditions were generally appalling, with long hours, low pay, inadequate accommodation and safety procedures and a punitive code of labour laws which heavily penalized breaches of industrial discipline. Trade unions and political parties were of course banned. It was the relative cheapness of labour in Russia, the highly profitable interest rates and the apparently stable political situation which were so attractive to foreign investors.

However, the rapid growth, dense concentration and the dangerous and insanitary working conditions of the industrial proletariat created a situation which was obviously conducive to the spread of mass discontent which soon expressed itself in the formation of group solidarity, strike movements, a highly-developed proletarian consciousness and increasing receptivity to the agitation and propaganda of revolutionary activists. Among these were more and more who, attracted by the theories of Karl Marx and Friedrich Engels, had begun to see the industrial working class, rather than the peasantry, as the major vehicle for revolutionary change in Russia. It is against this background of continuing political reaction, industrial expansion and the development of capitalist relationships that the origins of Russian Marxism have to be traced.

4
Rebellion and constitution

Origins of Russian Marxism

The first self-styled Russian Marxist revolutionary group was founded in Switzerland in 1883. It called itself the Group for the Liberation of Labour, and was composed of only four people, all ex-populists: George Plekhanov (1856–1918), Paul Axelrod (1850–1928), Leo Deutsch (1855–1941) and Vera Zasulich (1851–1919). It would be wrong, however, to believe that Marxism was unknown in Russia before that date. Indeed, it was familiarity with Marx's analysis of the political economy of industrial capitalism in Europe that had led many of the populists to seek an alternative, Russian path to socialism. However, as faith in the revolutionary potential of the peasantry began to fade, increasing numbers of radical intellectuals and, later, industrial workers in Russia became 'converted' to Marxism. As capitalism and industrialization progressed, they gradually adopted Marx's view that society must first pass from the feudal through the capitalist stage of development before the revolutionary proletariat could overthrow its 'bourgeois' government and establish a socialist workers' state. There were, however, problems with this theory as applied to Russia. As we know, Russia was an autocratic state with no political freedom, no economically powerful, politically conscious middle class (bourgeoisie), and a tiny undeveloped proletariat. At first, therefore, it seemed inappropriate to think in terms of a 'bourgeois-democratic', still less a 'proletarian-socialist', revolution in Russia. However, the social and economic changes brought about by Witte's industrialization convinced the early Russian Marxists that they were right, that capitalism would displace feudalism, and that just as surely the Russian working class would eventually destroy capitalism. In fact Marx himself had not discounted the populist notion that the peasant *obshchina* might serve as the starting point for socialism in Russia, and he had great personal admiration for some populist theoreticians, especially Chernyshevsky. However, the members of Liberation of Labour, particularly Plekhanov, devoted their theoretical skills to repudiating the populists' case, arguing that the *obshchina* did not provide the model for a socialist society and that the development of capitalism leading to a proletarian socialist revolution in Russia was inevitable.

During the 1890s, as the Russian labour force grew in size and strength, there sprang up an increasing number of workers' organizations, embryonic trade unions, Marxist discussion circles and other groups which conducted both agitation and propaganda activities and helped to organize strikes in the major industrial centres. In 1898 an attempt was made to weld these various cells, regional organizations and committees into a united, revolutionary Marxist political party. In that year there took place the first 'Congress' of the Russian Social Democratic Labour Party (RSDRP), forerunner of the later Communist Party of the Soviet Union. Very little, however, was achieved at the Congress (there were only nine delegates) and the infant party's leadership was soon arrested and imprisoned. The 'party', therefore, had no formal organization, agreed programme, proper membership or central agencies and existed in name only. In 1903 a second attempt was made to forge a unified party, though what in fact occurred was the fateful division of the RSDRP into two major and ultimately irreconcilable factions, known as the Mensheviks and the Bolsheviks.

It was during the interval between the first and second congresses that a crucial role in the party's internal history began to be played by a young Marxist intellectual by the name of Vladimir Ilyich Ulyanov, better known by his pseudonym of Lenin (1870–1924). Lenin was in exile in Siberia at the time of the 1898 Congress, but while there he became increasingly perturbed by certain tendencies within the social-democratic movement, both in Russia and in Europe. First, he was alarmed at the 'revisionist' theories of the German social democrat, Eduard Bernstein, who suggested that the transition to socialism could be achieved without a workers' revolution. Second, Lenin criticized those within Russian social democracy who argued that the party should concentrate the workers' attention on the *economic* struggle against capitalism as the means of raising proletarian political consciousness. Lenin believed that this trend of 'economism' would encourage the workers to develop merely a 'trade-union consciousness' and distract them from the vital political task of overthrowing tsarism. In 1900 he left Siberia, travelled to Europe, and there, together with Plekhanov and company, founded a new revolutionary underground newspaper called *Iskra* ('The Spark') through the distribution of which he intended to fight the 'economist' heresy and develop a strong organizational party network. His views on party organization were further developed in his all-important pamphlet, published in 1902, entitled *What is to be Done?* In it he ridiculed the idea that the working class could by its own efforts spontaneously develop a socialist political consciousness, and argued that it was the party's task 'to divert the labour movement from the unconscious tendency of trade-unionism, and bring it under the influence of Social Democracy instead'. What was needed, he urged, was 'a party of a new type' that would not simply follow behind and reflect the interests of the workers, but would, on the contrary, form 'the vanguard of the proletariat'. It was above all Lenin's uncompromising stand on party organization, discipline and leadership outlined in *What is to be Done?* that was to cause the schism in the party at the second Congress in 1903.

One of the most important items on the Congress's agenda turned out to be the question of the criteria for party membership. Lenin's hitherto close comrade, Julius Martov (1873–1923), proposed that a party member must, first, accept the party programme; second, support the party financially; and, third, be prepared to work under the direction of one of the party organizations. Lenin agreed with the first two principles but objected to the third. In his formulation, a party member must work '*in* one of the party organizations'. It was only a slight variation in wording, but what might seem to be merely a semantic quibble in fact exposed two widely differing views as to what type of party there should be: the one envisaged a broad party of sympathetic supporters prepared to render 'personal co-operation' with party organizations; the other a narrow, disciplined party of fully committed activists. Lenin lost the vote. On a later item, however, which also concerned the question of party leadership and centralization, he won a slender majority – largely due to abstentions by his opponents. Armed with this fragile numerical superiority, Lenin promptly dubbed his supporters the 'majority-ites'. The Russian word for 'majority' is *bolshinstvo* – hence, *bolsheviki*. His opponents, led by Martov – despite actually becoming the larger section within the party – were called the 'minority-ites' or *mensheviki*. Although, for the moment, they were technically two factions of a single party, and despite several later attempts at reunification, the split between the Mensheviks and Bolsheviks proved permanent and irreparable.

It is, however, premature at this stage in the party's history to think of Bolshevism or of Marxist-Leninist theory as a coherent and fully developed ideology. Over the coming years both Lenin and the Mensheviks responded in different ways to different circumstances and events, and many issues of a tactical, ideological, practical and even financial nature contained to divide them. The lessons of the 1905 revolution; the question of participation or non-participation in the elections to the State Dumas; the debates over whether or not to 'liquidate' the underground party network once political parties were no longer illegal and whether or not to continue the practice of armed 'expropriations' to secure party funds; and, finally, the attitude to Russia's involvement in the First World War: all these were highly contentious and divisive issues which not only kept the two factions apart but also created sub-factions within factions. It is also a mistake to think of Lenin as being completely in control of Bolshevik theory and practice. True, he had great personal authority and an unshakeable belief in the correctness of his own position. He was not, however, either omnipotent or infallible, and he was certainly not regarded by his colleagues as the party 'leader' in the full sense of the term. In any case, apart from a brief spell when he returned to Russia in 1905, he spent the years before 1917 mostly abroad and was therefore cut off from the everyday organizational activity of party workers on the ground in Russian towns and factories. Right up until the October 1917 Revolution – and beyond – Lenin had constantly to argue, persuade, cajole or even threaten in order to make his point or defend a thesis. It was only after his death in 1924 that 'Leninism' became transformed into something approaching holy writ. However, despite its initially shapeless and inchoate nature, Bolshevism had been born. The world-shaking implications of its obscure nativity had yet to be realized.

1905

The political atmosphere inside Russia at the time of the second Congress of the RSDRP was highly charged. The Social Democrats (SDs) were not the only party to try to get themselves organized. In 1900 the neo-populist Socialist-Revolutionary Party (SRs) was founded at Kharkov in Ukraine. Its programme reflected the aspirations of the earlier *narodniki*, including social revolution, redistribution of the land and retention of the peasant commune. It also shared the *Narodnaya volya*'s belief in the efficacy of political terror, and the party's 'fighting squads' began to carry out a wave of spectacular political assassinations, their victims including two Ministers of the Interior and one Prime Minister. Political opposition to autocracy was not, however, the monopoly of the extreme left. At the accession of Nicholas II (r. 1894–1917), representatives of the *zemstva* began to revive calls for a constitution. The new tsar dismissed these as 'senseless dreams', but around the turn of the century *zemstva* politicians and members of certain professional societies attempted to give some organizational shape to Russia's emerging liberal movement by founding the Union of Liberation, a body which rejected revolutionary activity, but called for the end of autocratic government and the establishment of a constitutional democracy based on representative institutions and the rule of law.

After four decades of relative calm the dormant Russian countryside began to stir once more and finally erupted in a series of violent upheavals (1901–7) whose origins lay in the injustices of the emancipation settlement. These were seen as the years of the 'red cockerel' – an image which was used to symbolize the regular sight of burning manor-houses put to the torch by the resentful and newly aroused peasantry. The strike movement continued in the factories, workers' grievances now fuelled by the economic depression which set in after the Witte boom. In the Far East, war had broken out between Russia and Japan. After a short burst of patriotic enthusiasm the war became unpopular, its motives misunderstood, and the naval and military blunders which attended its conduct became a further stimulus to anti-government feeling. All this represented a volatile mixture which needed only a spark to ignite an explosion. It was provided, significantly, by the workers of St Petersburg. On Sunday 9 January 1905 a peaceful protest march of striking factory workers and their families ended in bloody massacre. The demonstrators, led by a priest, had planned to present a humble petition to the tsar listing their grievances; instead they were met with a fusillade of bullets and charged down by mounted Cossacks. Hundreds died, and the butchery of 'Bloody Sunday' shocked the world. The revulsion following the slaughter soon engulfed the whole nation and there were widespread manifestations of popular grief, indignation and anger against the guilty tsar. Not just the industrial workers but the middle classes, professional organizations, intellectuals and the whole of Russian society were roused to fury. The tsar, typically, did nothing until the assassination in February of his uncle, Grand-Duke Sergei, finally impelled him to issue a decree authorizing the election of a consultative assembly. The announcement was sadly inadequate to respond to the popular mood and only served to spur both liberals and revolutionaries to intensify their activities and raise the level of their demands. Universal suffrage, a constituent assembly with full legislative powers, and the introduction of constitutionally guaranteed civil liberties now comprised their minimal programme. Unrest was reaching out to the villages and, menacingly, to the armed services. Military and naval mutinies flared up and now seriously called into question the automatic loyalty of the military to the regime. Recent research has shown that the political disaffection of the Russian army in 1905 was far more widespread than has been traditionally supposed – and provided an ominous portent for the events of 1917.

The promulgation in August of a manifesto containing details of the assembly promised in February was ignored by a Russian public whose temper and expectations had radically altered since the carnage of Bloody Sunday. Towards the end of September a fresh upsurge of industrial unrest soon spread from the Moscow railworkers to other sectors of the economy, paralysed communications and rapidly brought the administration of the whole country grinding to a halt. The helpless regime was now in the grip of Russia's first political general strike, the most powerful weapon in the arsenal of civil disobedience.

There was, however, no organized leadership, no centrally coordinated plan of action, no universally agreed programme of reform behind the movement. The Great October Strike was a spontaneous expression of the whole people's pent-up frustration at the obstinacy of an intellectually and administratively bankrupt regime. An extremely important by-product of the general strike was the formation of a democratically elected workers' 'parliament' which represented the interests of the striking workers in the capital and enjoyed the support of most of the revolutionary parties. This was the short-lived St Petersburg *Soviet* (Council) of Workers' Deputies, an institution which was destined to play a crucial role in Russia's future history and add a new word to the political vocabulary of the world. The publication of its first news-sheet, called *Izvestiya* ('News'), on 17 October coincided with the promulgation of a fresh imperial decree which promised to satisfy the enhanced demands for political reform referred to above. The October Manifesto granted full civil liberties, extended the franchise and ordered immediate elections to a State Duma. It appeared to be a triumph for the forces of democratic change. The tsar was personally not enthusiastic, the revolutionary parties treated it with scepticism, but a major concession had been made.

The concession was, however, tempered by a new determination on the government's part to crush the continuing rebellions and bring the country finally to heel. Punitive expeditions flogged the peasantry into submission; strikes were countered with lock-outs; gangs of ultra-nationalist thugs called the Black Hundreds beat up students, strikers and Jews; and on 3 December the members of the St Petersburg Soviet were arrested, later to be tried, imprisoned and exiled. The so-called 'Days of Freedom' were over. But one last, violent act in the tragedy of 1905 had yet to be played out. In December an armed uprising of Moscow workers was brutally suppressed after weeks of murderous urban warfare and a devastating artillery bombardment of the workers' homes and factories. Hundreds died in the fighting and many more were summarily shot after perfunctory street courts-martial. The suppression of the Moscow rising marked the end of the immediate revolutionary situation – although peace did not return to the countryside for a further two years. The convulsions of 1905, however, cannot be described as a revolution in the full sense of the term. They did not bring about any real devolution of political power, which still rested in the hands of a pusillanimous emperor and his personally chosen ministers; there was no redistribution of wealth or property; society was not restructured; and the powers of the bureaucracy, military and police remained unaltered. The revolutionary parties were in disarray and uncertain how to operate in the unfamiliar circumstances of Duma politics. Their leaders were either in prison, exile or abroad and were in any event locked in acrimonious doctrinal and organizational disputes. This is why Lenin described the events of 1905 not as a revolution, but as a 'dress rehearsal for revolution'. Rehearsal over, the stage was now set for the drama of 1917.

'Constitutional' politics, 1906–16

Between 1905 and 1917, having survived its first confrontation with the revolutionary masses since the Pugachev revolt, the imperial regime now entered into a period of uneasy and ambiguous experimentation with quasi-constitutional politics. Article 4 of the new Fundamental Laws, published on 23 April 1906, stated that 'Supreme Autocratic power belongs to the Emperor of All Russia', and article 9 that 'no law can come into existence without His approval'. The sovereign emperor also had full charge of foreign policies, the armed services and all government appointments. While the power of the autocracy, therefore, remained intact, two new institutions were established, the State Council and the State Duma, which were designed to allow public participation in both the deliberative and the legislative processes of policy-making at government level. The Duma consisted of around 500 elected deputies from all classes of Russian society, and the State Council (a kind of 'upper house') contained an equal proportion of elected and appointed representatives of the major social, religious, educational and financial institutions.

The newly legalized political parties entitled to put up candidates for election to the Duma covered the whole political spectrum from the Bolsheviks, Mensheviks and SRs on the left to the extreme right-wing, proto-fascist and anti-Semitic Union of the Russian People. In the centre, the major liberal party was the Constitutional Democratic Party (*Kadets*), and, slightly to its right, the Union of 17 October (Octobrists), a moderate conservative party which based its programme on the October 1905 manifesto. The SDs and SRs boycotted the elections to the first Duma and its composition was consequently dominated by the *Kadets* and a radical–liberal coalition called the Labour Group (*Trudoviki*). Over 200 deputies were peasants who failed to display the loyal conservatism expected of them by the government. The extreme right failed to gain a single seat. Despite the absence of the socialists, the deliberations of the first Duma proved to be much too radical in tone and anti-government in orientation for the liking of the tsar and his reactionary Prime Minister, Goremykin. It was accordingly dissolved after only ten weeks of existence (27 April–8 July 1906) and a second Duma convened in February 1907. This was a much more polarized body than the first. The *Kadets* lost ground, while the lifting of the socialists' boycott increased left-wing representation. The right also made some gains. Once more, however, the government of the tsar and the assembly of the people found it impossible to work together, and an excuse was engineered to bring about the dismissal of the second Duma in June 1907. At this point the new, tough Prime Minister, Peter Stolypin (1862–1911) – in flagrant violation of the Fundamental Laws – altered the electoral procedures by narrowing the franchise in favour of the landed nobility and the wealthy urban classes at the expense of the peasants and workers. This high-handed and dictatorial action ensured that the third Duma, when it convened, was of an altogether different political complexion from its predecessors. The Octobrists, who had had only seventeen deputies in the first Duma, now had 154. The extreme right also increased its share of the vote and the Social Democrats and *Trudoviki* were reduced to a rump. The third Duma therefore proved to be a much more conservative and compliant assembly which could be more or less relied on to rubber-stamp government policies and stifle the few elements of radicalism left in its midst. Even this Duma was, however, temporarily suspended on occasion while the government forced through new legislation by decree. The fact that the deputies meekly resumed their seats after the suspension was lifted is a measure of their malleability – a factor which ensured the survival of the third Duma throughout its allotted five-year span (1907–12).

The life of the third Duma coincided roughly with the premiership of Stolypin, a man whose unimpeachably loyalist sympathies were combined with a vigorous commitment to the need for agrarian reform. The convulsions in the Russian countryside between 1901 and 1907 convinced Stolypin that, nearly half a century after the emancipation, the peasant land question was still one of the most urgent problems for the government to tackle. It is not necessary to dwell on the fine details of his legislation. Its central feature was an attempt to break what Stolypin regarded as the dead-grip of the peasant commune on agricultural productivity. Accordingly, in what he himself described as a deliberate 'wager on the sturdy and the strong', Stolypin authorized the consolidation of scattered allotment land, abolished compulsory communal land-tenure and encouraged the establishment of individually owned farmsteads which were 'cut out' of the collective land. Redemption payments were cancelled, the legal status of peasants improved, and financial support was given to encourage the already growing movement of peasant migration from European Russia to the rich agricultural lands of western and southern Siberia. It is difficult to gauge the success of Stolypin's reform. The legal, bureaucratic and financial complexity of the operation bedevilled it from the start, and it is impossible to calculate what the long-term effects might have been had not more cataclysmic events thrown the whole land issue once more into the melting-pot in 1917. Stolypin's 'wager on the strong' certainly benefited some of the richer peasants (the so-called *kulaks*) but did very little to alleviate the distress of the poorer villagers still suffering from shortage of land. This served to increase the economic differentials within the peasant class, the rich becoming richer and the poor poorer. The major deficiency was, however, Stolypin's failure to tackle the agrarian problem as a whole. His legislation dealt only with peasant land and did nothing to touch the property interests or the private estates of the landed gentry. This was an issue which the peasants themselves were to address by direct action in the turmoil of 1917.

The elections to the fourth and final Duma resulted in the return of an even more conservative membership than that of the third, with the Octobrists losing votes to the more extreme right-wing nationalist parties. However, it was during the lifetime of this last Duma that certain developments took place which served to open a breach not only between the government and the Duma, but also between government and society as a whole. In 1911 Stolypin was murdered by a Socialist-Revolutionary assassin (who was at the same time a police agent). In the following year the massacre of 200 striking workers at the Lena goldfields in eastern Siberia aroused public indignation and provoked a renewed outbreak of politically motivated industrial unrest which mounted in intensity over the next two years. 1912 was also the year in which the political impact began to be felt of the emperor's and empress's personal patronage of their bizarre 'friend', Grigory Rasputin (1871–1916). Rasputin was not, as he is often described, a 'mad monk' but a member of an extreme religious sect of flagellants in Siberia known as *khlysty*. He was also uncouth, a drunkard and a lecher, who was nevertheless lionized by certain sections, particularly the ladies, of St Petersburg's high society. The royal couple, however, regarded him as a holy 'man of the people' sent to them by God to save the dynasty by his seemingly miraculous ability to cure the haemophiliac bleeding of the heir to the throne, the young tsarevich Alexis. Through his hypnotic healing powers Rasputin exercised a powerful hold over the tsar and was thereby able – in return for sexual favours arranged for him by ambitious politicians – to influence the emperor's choice of government ministers. There is probably no substance in the allegations that Rasputin had sexual relations with the empress, but his outrageous public behaviour and his intimacy with the royal family succeeded in bringing the court, and with it the government, into public disrepute. Though they were not all, of course, Rasputin nominees, ministers of the crown were hired and fired in rapid succession in what has been described as a game of 'ministerial leap-frog'. Between 1912 and 1916 Russia had four Prime Ministers, four Ministers of Justice, four of

Education, four Procurators of the Holy Synod and no less than six Ministers of the Interior, all of them, in Professor Florinsky's words, 'pebbles – not milestones – on the road that led the monarchy to ruin'. Rasputin was eventually poisoned and shot to death by a member of the royal family, Prince Felix Yusupov, in December 1916. Two months later the autocracy collapsed, but the scandal which had surrounded Rasputin's name was merely a symptom, not a cause, of the acute malaise which afflicted an incompetent and unpopular regime now deep in the throes of a devastating international war.

5
War and revolution

Russia at war, 1914 to February 1917

The nature of the relationship between Russia's involvement in the First World War and the 1917 Revolution is a topic which has been mulled over by historians ever since the events took place. Put very simply, the question boils down to this: did the military situation generate the domestic crisis which brought about the disintegration of the tsarist regime; or were the pressures and contradictions within the social and political system already of such a refractory nature as to make revolution in any case inevitable? Against those who argue that it was the war which caused – or at any rate accelerated – the Revolution, it can be countered that the domestic situation before August 1914 was already reaching crisis point. The widespread industrial unrest following the Lena goldfield shootings, the deteriorating relations between the government and the Duma, the political disaffection of the middle classes and the repercussions of the Rasputin affair, and the unresolved agrarian problems – all suggested that state and society were once more lurching towards some kind of dramatic confrontation. The declaration of war between Russia and Germany, however, temporarily defused the situation as a wave of primitive patriotism swept across the country impelling tsar, government, society and the people to unite briefly in the defence of Mother Russia. Only the

Social Democrats, and then not all of them, opposed the 'imperialist' war – a situation from which the Bolsheviks were to draw dividends as the popular mood later swung away from one of optimistic and aggressive nationalism to war-weariness and a yearning for Russia's unilateral withdrawal.

Russia's crushing defeat at the battle of Tannenberg in August 1914 set the pattern for future hostilities, but it is the repercussions of the conflict on the domestic front, rather than the military operations, which directly concern us here. Economically, the effects of the war were far-reaching. Industries producing war *matériel* obviously flourished. Huge fortunes were made out of government orders for guns, bullets and uniforms. When it became obvious that the war would not be over quickly, more and more enterprises converted to military and paramilitary production. On the other hand, output of consumer goods plummeted with consequent hardships for the civilian population. Even essential farming equipment was in short supply. These difficulties were compounded by problems of transportation. Most railway rolling-stock was commandeered to carry men and munitions to the front, leaving little to ferry much-needed foodstuffs from the grain-growing regions to the towns. Shortages ensued, workers went hungry and bread queues became a familiar sight. Undersupply of essential raw materials also meant that industry faced a crisis in 1915–16 which was partially overcome by the formation of the War Industries Committee, a voluntary organization of businessmen, Duma politicians and workers' committees which co-ordinated production and to some extent offset the government's increasingly obvious inability to cope efficiently with the economic strains of total war.

Financially, the country was heading for disaster. Naval blockades of the Baltic and Black Seas effectively cut off Russia's foreign trade. Overland commerce through eastern Europe was obviously impossible. Poland and large areas of western Russia were occupied by enemy troops, with consequent loss not only of industrial resources, but also of tax-paying population. Further self-inflicted injuries on the exchequer were caused by the early prohibition of alcohol sales. The sale of vodka was a lucrative source of state revenue which now literally dried up (not that the Russian peasants ceased drinking their own home-brewed and often lethal liquor). While revenues slumped, expenditure soared. The direct costs of the war leapt from around 1,500 million rubles in 1914 to 14,500 million in 1916. The government's expedient was heavy foreign borrowing and the printing of more paper rubles which resulted in galloping inflation. The mass mobilization of 15 million conscript troops between 1914 and 1917 also had obvious repercussions on the nation's economy. In the over-populated countryside the removal of so much superfluous manpower meant that there were fewer mouths to feed at home. The army, however, could not march on a stomach which was underfed. Conscription of agricultural labourers from the large private estates which produced mainly for the market resulted in reduced output at a time of increased demand. Labour productivity in industry also declined as skilled workers, already in short supply, were replaced with inexperienced labourers, women, children and prisoners-of-war.

Increasingly the population began to voice its discontent, not only with the military reverses, but also with the domestic hardships which were directly attributed – rightly or wrongly – to the government's incompetence. The short-lived mood of national solidarity at the outbreak of war had now evaporated. Industry was battered by a renewed wave of strikes, some of them financed by German money. Members of the centre parties in the Duma formed a political alliance called the 'Progressive Block' which called on the tsar to sack his obviously inept administration and replace it with a 'government of public confidence' – by which they presumably meant themselves. The War Industries Committee and other voluntary organizations such as the Union of *Zemstva* found their relief and welfare activities hampered rather than encouraged by officialdom, but a mixture of patriotism and profits derived from war-production prevented them from actually backing their political demands with economic threats or sanctions. The tsar foolishly added to his own isolation and unpopularity by assuming personal command of the Russian army in 1915. His unhelpful presence at military headquarters in Mogilev left the conduct of affairs in the capital (now renamed Petrograd as a 'patriotic' gesture) more in the hands of his neurotic wife – contemptuously known by the public as *nemka* ('the German woman') – and the abominable Rasputin.

Heavy losses at the front and enhanced conscription in the

rear meant that the complexion and the composition of the Russian army were changing. In the ranks the demoralized troops were not so much trained and loyal fighters for tsar and country as hastily drafted and poorly equipped 'peasants in uniform'. The traditional officer corps was also becoming increasingly diluted by the enrolment of young professional men who would otherwise never have contemplated a military career. These may perhaps be described as the 'intelligentsia in uniform' – a body whose political instincts were not predisposed to automatic fealty to the regime. At the top, even the general staff, exasperated by the inexperienced military meddling of an ineffectual emperor, were becoming alienated from their sovereign, and pressures began to build up for his resignation. Despite the disaffection of the military, however, it was neither the high command nor the Duma politicians, still less the revolutionary parties, which finally brought about the downfall of 'Bloody Nicholas'. It was caused by the spontaneous upsurge of the politically radicalized masses.

The February Revolution and 'dual power', February–July 1917

The crisis came to a head in late February 1917. Disturbances in food-lines of hungry shoppers soon escalated into violent demonstrations, clashes with the police and, ultimately, military mutiny among the restless troops garrisoned in the capital. Within four hectic days, 27 February to 2 March, the Duma was prorogued, the government collapsed, the tsar was forced to abdicate and there sprang into existence two new revolutionary organs of political authority, the first Provisional Government and the Petrograd Soviet of Workers' and Soldiers' Deputies. The autocracy was at an end. The Provisional (i.e. temporary) Government, headed by Prince Lvov, was dominated by *Kadets* and other members of the 'Progressive Bloc', and thus, although catapulted into government power by the action of the revolutionary workers and soldiers of Petrograd, represented the political interests of the middle and upper classes. In the few weeks of its existence it carried through a programme of democratic reforms and civil rights legislation which led even Lenin – its uncompromising opponent – to describe Russia as 'the freest of all the belligerent countries'. It was, however, the continuing belligerence of the new government's policy in pursuing the war which was soon to bring about its fall. The 'provisional' designation of Lvov's administration was thus borne out by events; whether it was ever truly a 'government' is open to question in view of the nature of its relationship with the Petrograd Soviet. Despite the unwieldy, chaotic and fluid nature of its composition, it was the Soviet, or rather its Central Executive Committee, which was in real charge of events in the capital. Both by the extent of popular support which it enjoyed and by its control of the factories, barracks and major modes of communication, the workers' Soviet became the effective co-government of Russia, an arrangement which was characterized by the term 'dual power' (*dvoevlastie*).

As the authority of the old tsarist bureaucracy and police force crumbled throughout the country, it was replaced by a bewildering number and variety of people's councils, soviets, committees and other organs of popular control which capitalized on the chaos by pursuing and protecting their own sectional and often mutually conflicting interests. The peasantry – apart from those in uniform – played no part in the February Revolution. However, as the year wore on the paralysis of the rural administration provided the opportunity for the peasants to realize their old dream and seize the land for the benefit of those who worked it. The agrarian disturbances ranged in seriousness from acts of trespass and illicit tree-chopping to the wholesale expropriation and redistribution of the large private estates and even the farms of those who had opted out of the communes under Stolypin's reforms. Violence, if necessary, was used. The government called for patience, order and proper legislative procedures following elections to a Constituent Assembly. The niceties of parliamentarianism, however, were lost on the semi-literate and land-hungry peasant who was finally achieving 'from below' what Alexander II had failed to implement 'from above' in 1861.

Even more urgent than the land question was the issue of war. Naturally no one wanted to be overrun by Germany and Austro-Hungary, but the overwhelming mood of the masses, in and out of uniform, was one of fatigue and a desire to end the slaughter. Military discipline was undermined by the Petrograd Soviet's 'Order No. 1', published on 2 March, which called for the setting up of soldiers' committees in every military unit and the abolition of traditionally hierarchical relationships between officers and men. Desertions, fraternization, and refusal to fight anything but a defensive war which would lead to a 'democratic peace' without 'annexations or indemnities' became increasingly common.

In the fields and factories and at the front, therefore, the population was mobilizing itself for continued revolutionary action as the twin organs of dual power hedged and havered on the two crucial issues of the day – peace and land. The situation within the revolutionary parties was no more clear-cut. Even the Bolsheviks (in Lenin's absence), rejoicing over the downfall of the monarchy, were prepared for a long, indefinite period of 'bourgeois' government and equivocal over the question of reunification with the Mensheviks. Things changed when Lenin arrived back in Russia on 3 April. At the Finland railway station in Petrograd he addressed the welcoming crowds with a ringing call for international socialist revolution. This surprised even some senior Bolsheviks who by and large were content with the accomplishment of the February, 'bourgeois', Revolution. They should, however, have had no reason for surprise. Ever since 1905 Lenin had been talking and writing about the establishment of a 'revolutionary democratic dictatorship of the proletariat and poor peasantry'. Now he wasted no time in elaborating his views in his celebrated *April Theses*, published in the party newspaper, *Pravda*, on 7 April. His sights were now firmly set on transforming the bourgeois-democratic revolution into a proletarian uprising and the inauguration of a socialist workers' state under the slogan of 'All Power to the Soviets'.

Lenin's attitude to the Soviets was in fact equivocal. On the one hand, they were an example of the kind of working-class 'spontaneity' of which he had always been suspicious and against which he had cautioned in *What is to be Done?* On the other hand, they now appeared to be much more representative of the interests of the working class than the liberal- and middle-class-dominated Provisional Government, and as such seemed to offer the best means of effecting the transition from the bourgeois-democratic to the proletarian-socialist revolution. Later the slogan was briefly discarded when leaders of the Petrograd Soviet seemed to be more concerned with furthering the policies of the Provisional Government – to the extent of accepting ministerial appointments – than of advancing the revolutionary cause of the masses. At the first All-Russian Congress of Soviets in June, Bolsheviks only accounted for about one-eighth of the total delegates. Only in September when the Bolsheviks had a clear majority on the Soviets in the capital and elsewhere, was the slogan revived and acted upon. For the time being the *April Theses* were not yet party policy and were indeed editorially repudiated in the columns of *Pravda*. Lenin's call for a workers' revolution was interpreted by many, even among his own supporters, as opportunist, adventurist, un-Marxist and as a dangerous slide into Bakuninist anarchism. However, despite the reservations of party intellectuals and theoreticians, Lenin's programme manifestly reflected and articulated the increasingly radical temper of the party rank-and-file and the militant workers and troops. By the end of April his *Theses* had become accepted as the immediate party programme, and over the next few months party membership soared, industrial workers accounting for 60 per cent of the increased membership. It could be argued that before April 1917 Lenin and the Bolsheviks were a relatively unimportant factor in Russian history. This was no longer the case. From its position in the wings of Russian politics the Bolshevik party was soon to take the centre of the stage.

On 18 April the publication of a note from the Foreign Minister, Milyukov, assuring the Allies that Russia would fight the war to victory led to angry public protests and ultimately to the resignation of Lvov's government. A new administration was formed which now included members of the socialist parties in the Soviet. The 'collaboration' of Menshevik and SR ministers with the bourgeois, pro-war government meant that the Bolsheviks were now the only political faction which pursued an unswervingly anti-war policy, Lenin urging the transformation of the imperialist war into a series of revolutionary wars within each belligerent country. The firm expectation of international revolution in Europe was uppermost in his mind when the Bolsheviks launched their own revolution in October.

In June, the new Minister for War, Alexander Kerensky (1881–1971), vice-chairman of the Soviet and a moderate socialist, ordered a new military offensive against Austria on the Galician front. The initial advance was checked and rapidly turned into a rout. The military catastrophe was matched by a fresh outbreak of public disorders in Petrograd. Thousands of demonstrators thronged the streets; Bolshevik banners abounded; many people were killed or injured; the socialist Minister of Agriculture was nearly lynched. The 'July Days' were the most menacing manifestation of popular discontent with government since the February Revolution. Lenin, however, judged that it was premature for the demonstrations to escalate into revolution, and a semblance of civic order was restored. Bolshevik fortunes now took a brief downward turn. The Soviet's participation in the second Provisional Government and the numerical superiority of its Menshevik and SR membership led Lenin temporarily to abandon the slogan of 'All Power to the Soviets'. Kerensky became the new Prime Minister while the ultra-disciplinarian General Kornilov was appointed Commander-in-Chief and reintroduced capital punishment at the front. Rumours were spread that Lenin was a German agent in the Kaiser's pay, and orders went out for his arrest. Bolsheviks were blamed both for the violence of the July uprising and for the failure of the Galician offensive through spreading anti-war propaganda at the front. Mutinous regiments were disbanded and Bolshevik newspapers banned. Lenin eluded arrest and went to ground in Finland. Among the other Bolsheviks placed under arrest was Leo Trotsky. Always something of a maverick in the Social Democratic movement, Trotsky headed his own independent organization but now, having returned to Russia from abroad in May, he declared his solidarity with the Bolsheviks. He was soon to play a leading role in the planning and execution of the October Revolution.

Despite the new government's display of firmness, problems continued to multiply. Rural revolt, the breakdown of industry, military collapse, rampant inflation and movements for national independence in Finland, Poland, Ukraine and the Caucasus added to the turbulent tide of revolution swirling around Kerensky's boots. Reluctance to tackle the land problem, procrastination over convening a Constituent Assembly and, above all, the continuation of the war clearly demonstrated the legalistically-minded Prime Minister's failure to respond effectively to the revolutionary mood of the masses. Only the Bolsheviks promised immediate 'Peace, Bread and Land'.

Towards the Bolshevik Revolution, August–October 1917

The immediate threat to Kerensky did not, however, come from the left but from the right in the shape of General Kornilov's attempted military coup launched on 28 August. Relations between the Prime Minister and his Commander-in-Chief were a mixture of political antagonism and personal mistrust. Steady German advances through the Baltic region, culminating in the capture of Riga on 21 August, opened the enemy's path to Petrograd, and Kornilov had no faith in Kerensky's ability to take the tough political measures necessary to halt the military reverses. Suspecting Kornilov of planning to seize political power, Kerensky relieved him of his command. Ignoring this, Kornilov retaliated by issuing his own proclamation and ordered Cossack and cavalry regiments to advance on the capital. Among other things he contemplated shooting the members of the Soviet. A counter-revolutionary military dictatorship seemed to be in the offing. His troops were, however, bewildered and uncertain of their loyalties, and in any case impeded in their progress by the disruptive action of railwaymen and workers from Petrograd who mingled with Kornilov's men and convinced them that their general's plan was against the interests of the revolution. Not a shot was fired. The dispirited troops dispersed and the counter-revolutionary *putsch* was aborted.

The real significance of the Kornilov 'mutiny' lies in the fact that it heralded a renewed upsurge of Bolshevik party popularity. The embattled Kerensky had been forced to appeal for its support; imprisoned socialist leaders were released and some right-wing politicians arrested. On 1 September Russia was declared a republic. The Soviet began to rearm detachments of factory-workers – the 'Red Guards' – and by early September the Bolsheviks for the first time gained a majority on the Petrograd and Moscow Soviets. Lenin, still in hiding, now revived the slogan 'All Power to the Soviets'. Over the next few weeks he bombarded the party's Central Committee with a barrage of demands for an *immediate* insurrection of the armed proletariat, the overthrow of 'Kerensky and Company', and the seizure of political power. Only a Bolshevik government, he argued, could satisfy the demands of the revolutionary people. Sweeping aside the hesitation of his comrades who counselled patience and wished to wait for elections to a Constituent

Assembly, or at least the planned meeting of the second Congress of Soviets, Lenin retorted, 'History will not forgive us if we do not take power now', and 'to delay is a crime'.

Trotsky, now released from gaol, was both chairman of the Petrograd Soviet and a member of the Bolshevik Central Committee. On 10 October Lenin left his hiding-place and made his way incognito to a meeting of the Central Committee. After protracted and often acrimonious debate his motion calling for armed insurrection was eventually approved by ten votes to two. The proletarian revolution was now 'the order of the day'. Which day, however, remained to be resolved. Lenin pushed for immediate action, but his return to hiding kept him from the epicentre of the threatening storm. More influential was Trotsky, now appointed chairman of a newly formed body, responsible to the Soviet, called the Military Revolutionary Committee, which effectively controlled the Petrograd garrison troops in open defiance of the Provisional Government and of Kerensky who had assumed supreme military command. The Bolsheviks made no secret of their preparations for insurrection, but Kerensky seemed impotent to stop it. Attempts to prosecute members of the Military Revolutionary Committee, close down the Bolshevik press and draft in loyal troops proved ineffectual.

It would, however, be incorrect to consider that the Bolsheviks' planning for revolution was efficient, co-ordinated or thoroughly considered. It succeeded by default rather than design. On Trotsky's own admission, the events of 24–26 October were marked by confusion, apprehension, uncertainty and opportunism. Lenin arrived at Bolshevik headquarters on the evening of the 24th. During the night detachments of armed workers, under orders of the Bolshevik-dominated Military Revolutionary Committee and commanded by party 'commissars' took over the nerve centres of the city. Unopposed, they occupied the railway stations, manned the bridges and seized the banks, post- and central telegraph offices. On the following day the Winter Palace – ex-home of the tsar and final refuge of the Provisional Government – was invested by Red Guards, soldiers and sailors. After hours of indecision and ignored ultimata punctuated by sporadic and innocuous shell-fire, the Palace was infiltrated (not 'stormed') during the night of the 25/26th by a squadron of revolutionary guards who arrested the remaining members of the Provisional Government. Kerensky was not among them. He had earlier fled in a car placed at his disposal by the United States Embassy. Such, briefly, were the relatively unspectacular main events of the politically momentous October Revolution. Only a dozen or so people lost their lives during the course of a forty-eight-hour crisis which was dramatically to alter the political history of the world.

Shortly before the arrest of the Provisional Government, the delegates to the belated second Congress of Soviets had begun their deliberations. The Bolsheviks were in any case in a majority, but the decision of the Mensheviks and right SRs to withdraw in protest at the announcement of the coup ensured that the action would be formally endorsed by Congress. Events had fortuitously fallen in with Trotsky's tactics, giving the outward appearance that the seizure of power by the Bolsheviks was in fact an assumption of power by the Soviets. At a later session the Congress also unanimously approved two crucial resolutions, the Decree on Peace and the Decree on Land, the former calling for an immediate armistice and a negotiated peace settlement, the second more or less rubber-stamping the process of land-redistribution which the peasants had in any case already accomplished by their own efforts. The Bolsheviks had thereby redeemed – on paper at least – the two major promises on which they had campaigned and which had clinched their mass support. Congress also established a new revolutionary government, consisting entirely of Bolsheviks with Lenin as chairman – the Soviet of People's Commissars (*Sovnarkom*). The first Soviet government had been born.

In the space of only eight months the Russian Empire, ruled by an absolute monarchy, had been dramatically transformed into a revolutionary republic headed by a government of Marxists dedicated to the establishment of international socialism. Lenin himself had leapt from relative obscurity to the leadership of that government. The Bolsheviks had successfully achieved power, but the Revolution had really only just begun. Their position was by no means secure; they were still a minority party; large sections of society either opposed them or were ignorant of their intentions; the conflict with Germany still ground on, soon to be superseded by an agonizing, fratricidal Civil War which spilled oceans of blood and created conditions of unspeakable chaos and suffering. Despite the immediate struggles and uncertainties, however, the Bolshevik Revolution of October 1917 had opened a new chapter in the history, not just of Russia, but of the entire planet.

Was the Revolution inevitable? Could it have been avoided or prevented? The question is of course purely hypothetical, and the historiographical and philosophical issues involved in an attempt to answer it are far too complex and profound to be tackled at this juncture. One point, however, is worth considering. There was clearly much more behind the Bolsheviks' victory than ideological or organizational superiority over other political forces. The Bolsheviks were simply much more in tune with popular feeling than either the constitutionally-minded liberal politicians or the moderate socialists. In particular, Lenin's resolute stand on peace and land and his appreciation of the revolutionary power of the peasantry contributed greatly to his party's popularity and its ultimate success. Of course, if Kerensky had adopted a similar programme; if he had held out the promise of an immediate end to the war and been prepared to give legislative effect to the redistribution of non-peasant land, then it is just possible that he would have gained the mass support needed to stay in power. But as Florinsky has pointed out, if Kerensky had espoused such a policy, then Kerensky, too would have been a Bolshevik.

6

Interpretations and conclusions

The Revolution promised, even if in the medium term it did not achieve, a resolution of the social, economic and political contradictions described in the opening chapter. It also marked the culmination of the earlier revolutionary traditions which combined the forces of popular insurrection, intellectual opposition and military defection, and in which elements of Westernism, Slavophilism, Populism, Marxism and anarchism could be identified. Not surprisingly, the highly charged political nature of the events of 1917 has given rise to a wide variety of interpretations and historiographical approaches which span the entire ideological and intellectual spectrum.

In the former Soviet Union, a strictly orthodox Marxist-Leninist (that is to say Stalinist) approach predominated – was indeed obligatory – in the interpretation of Revolution. According to this view, the October Revolution was the inevitable climax of a process of historical development governed by scientific laws, inexorable economic forces and the dynamics of class struggle. The Russian working class was led to victory in this struggle by the Bolshevik Party – the 'vanguard of the proletariat' – with Vladimir Ilyich Lenin at its head. 'The Great October Socialist Revolution' ushered in a new era in the history of mankind, the era of Socialism, which would in turn develop into full Communism. From the late 1920s until the late 1980s all professional historians, researchers, writers, teachers and students of the

50

Revolution inside the USSR were compelled to operate within this ideological and methodological framework which condemned all other interpretations as 'deviationist', 'counter-revolutionary', 'white-guardist', 'bourgeois-reactionary' and generally 'unscientific'. The writing of history thereby played a legitimizing role in the monopoly of political power enjoyed until recently by the Communist Party of the Soviet Union. History was the handmaiden of the State.

In the west, too, interpretations of the Revolution have also been coloured by political expediency and considerations which are not without their own ideological sub-text. At the time of the Revolution, knowledge in the west of the political, social and economic forces which had brought it about was minuscule. Bolshevism itself was an unknown quantity, and it is the unknown which usually excites the greatest fear. Foreign governments were understandably hostile to the infant socialist state whose leaders were openly committed to the goal of international revolution and the destruction of capitalism. A contemporary British politician, Winston Churchill, declared that Bolshevism must be 'strangled in its cradle'. But apart from political antipathy, cultural and even linguistic obstacles caused early western perceptions of the Revolution to be heavily influenced by the translated accounts, memoirs and analyses of Russian émigré writers and scholars – some of them leading, though losing, actors in the drama – who of course had their own personal and political axes to grind in their opposition to the Soviet regime. A 'liberal' counter-orthodoxy became established which postulated that, had it not been for the intervention of the First World War, Russia would have continued along a reformist road to greater political freedom, real constitutional government and economic prosperity. Some commentators, intellectually unable to admit that oppressive governments are on occasion overthrown by the spontaneous action of the masses, questioned whether a revolution in the proper sense of the term actually did occur in February 1917! According to this line of thinking, most controversially articulated by George Katkov, the abdication of Nicholas Romanov was precipitated by a conspiracy orchestrated by a 'freemasonry' of self-seeking businessmen and treacherous liberal politicians, and by the machinations of the German Foreign Office and military High Command, which financially underwrote the subversion of

Russia's war effort as part of their *Revolutionierungspolitik*, that is the policy of fomenting social and economic unrest in the enemy country. Others argue that once the war-battered regime *had* collapsed, the opportunity for establishing full civil freedoms and parliamentary institutions was greatly enhanced in Russia, and that, when the war was over, the country was set fair to develop along the lines of western-style democratic politics, a pluralistic civil society, the rule of law and a successful capitalist economy. The optimistic scenario was then undermined by the appearance on mid-stage of the wicked Bolsheviks, who, led by a dogmatic and power-thirsty zealot, hoodwinked the gullible masses and snatched political power at gunpoint, thereby inaugurating a reign of ideologically motivated terror which plunged Russia into a new Dark Age of totalitarian oppression. There have even been some contemptible efforts to explain the Revolution as a Jewish plot.

Whatever their claims to 'objectivity', the most influential representatives of western liberal scholarship in the mid-twentieth century continued to analyse the Revolution 'from above'. That is to say, they concentrated their studies on the activities of leading individuals (e.g. Nicholas II, Kerensky, Lenin) or principal groupings – such as the Fourth Duma, the Petrograd Soviet, the Provisional Governments, the Bolshevik Central Committee and so on – without undertaking a proper analysis of what the ordinary people of Russia – factory workers, land-hungry peasants, conscript soldiers, radicalized sailors, women in bread-queues – were thinking and doing in 1917. In the words of E. H. Carr, speaking in 1961 of recent western scholarship on Russia:

> Much of what has been written in English-speaking countries during the last ten years . . . has been vitiated by this inability to achieve even the most elementary measure of imaginative understanding of what goes on in the mind of the other party.

Those foreign writers, left-wing intellectuals and so-called 'fellow-travellers' who did try to evince some sympathy and understanding for the popular movements and elemental forces unleashed during the Revolution were often guilty of painting exaggeratedly glowing pictures of a nation which had overthrown tyranny and was now struggling to build a just and equitable society in which the interests of the toiling masses, rather than those of the exploiting classes, were the principal consideration. Their accounts, although well-intentioned, were often naïve and ill-informed. They were also condemned by both orthodox Marxists and western liberals: the former because those interpretations often laid too much emphasis on the spontaneous, popular nature of the Revolution, and not enough on the vanguard role of the Bolshevik Party; and the latter because they offered a vision of the common man able to take charge of his own destiny – an uncomfortable concept for many representatives of the traditional western 'establishment' to grasp.

Since E. H. Carr delivered his lecture, quoted from above, a new generation of western historians, less beholden to the old 'émigré–liberal' school, but still rejecting the institutionalized falsehoods of Soviet-style historical writing, has conducted an impressive amount of research and published a formidable array of works in which the Revolution has been investigated using a combination of traditional historiography, economic analysis, sociological enquiry and the methodology of political science. What has emerged is a refreshingly dispassionate and meticulously documented view of the Revolution 'from below' which demonstrates the full social complexity, the fluctuating rhythm, and the regional variety of the cataclysm which overtook the Russian Empire in 1917. Much of this research demonstrates that after the collapse of the autocracy, rather than unifying in some kind of common purpose, Russian society became increasingly polarized along class lines, with the workers, peasants and conscript soldiers becoming more and more alienated from a government which continued to defend the interests of the propertied classes. Lenin's slogan of 'All Power to the Soviets', adopted in April and revived on the eve of October, simply articulated the feeling of the *hoi polloi* that a government of the Soviets – the elected representatives of the plebeian masses – rather than a government of self-appointed middle- and upper-class conservative politicians and financially privileged businessmen was the preferred alternative. The American historian, Ronald Suny, has put it as follows:

The Bolsheviks came to power, not because they were superior manipulators or cynical opportunists, but because their policies, as formulated by Lenin in April and shaped by the events of the following months, placed them at the head of a genuinely popular movement.

On the other hand, another prominent American scholar, Richard Pipes, has recently written:

The Russian Revolution was made neither by the forces of nature nor by anonymous masses but by identifiable men pursuing their own advantages.

The controversy over the origins of the Russian Revolution, therefore, still continues unabated, and no less acrimoniously since the disintegration of the State which it engendered. Inside Russia itself, the breakdown of Communist Party control over the historiography of the Revolution has opened up a new vista of opportunities and created a whole gamut of fresh interpretations which, based on recently released archive material, offers exciting prospects for further study of 1917 and its antecedents. During the late 1980s, it became increasingly apparent that the traditional Marxist-Leninist orthodoxy was no longer acceptable. Society and the mass media ran ahead of the professional historical establishment in demanding a complete break from the half-truths and official gobbledegook of the past. Many erstwhile Communist historians now suddenly turned 'democrat', and joined in the often unseemly rush into resurrecting fallen idols of the old regime, into rehabilitating dishonoured figures of the past, and plunged into a wave of misplaced nostalgia for the symbols and totems of the historically bankrupt tsarist social and political order. The return of the imperial double-headed eagle (now uncrowned) as Russia's national symbol, the renaming of St Petersburg in 1991 (known as Leningrad since 1924), the rise of Russian nationalism, the upsurge of Orthodox Christianity, and even the renaissance of Romanov–monarchist sympathies in the ex-USSR are all symptomatic of a new, and not necessarily helpful, reinterpretation of Russia's pre-revolutionary and revolutionary history, the contours of which have yet to emerge in clearly identifiable relief. What is important, for both western and Russian scholars, is that the central importance of the Russian Revolutions of 1917 in shaping the history of the twentieth century should not be marginalized as a result of these ephemeral, and emotional, political trends. In condemning the political aftermath of the

1917 Revolution, its detractors should be careful not to misinterpret or wilfully ignore the misery and degradation, as well as the aspirations and ideals, of the Russian people which were its driving force.

Suggestions for further reading

The literature on the Russian Revolution is vast, running to thousands of volumes in English alone. The following is a highly selective list of suggestions. Extensive bibliographies and reference to further material will be found in many of these works. A new section has been added to take account of recent publications that have appeared since the first edition of this pamphlet was published.

Reference

H. Shukman (ed.), *The Blackwell Encyclopaedia of the Russian Revolution* (Oxford, 1987).

Anthologies of translated documents

R. V. Daniels (ed.), *The Russian Revolution* (New Jersey, 1972).

B. Dmytryshyn (ed.), *Imperial Russia: A Source Book* (Illinois, 1974).

M. McCauley (ed.), *The Russian Revolution and the Soviet State, 1917–1921: Documents* (London, 1975).

M. McCauley (ed.), *Octobrists to Bolsheviks: Imperial Russia, 1905–1917* (London, 1984).

M. McCauley and P. Waldron (eds), *The Emergence of the Modern Russian State, 1855–1881* (London, 1988).

General works on late Imperial Russia

M. Florinsky, *Russia: A History and an Interpretation*, vol. II (New York, 1966).

R. H. McNeal (ed.), *Russia in Transition, 1905–1914: Evolution or Revolution?* (London, 1980).

R. Pipes, *Russia under the Old Regime* (London, 1974).

H. Rogger, *Russia in the Age of Modernisation and Revolution* (London, 1983).

General histories of the revolutionary period

W. Chamberlin, *The Russian Revolution* (New York, 1935).

S. Fitzpatrick, *The Russian Revolution, 1917–32* (Oxford, 1982; reprinted 1987).

M. Florinsky, *The End of the Russian Empire* (New York, 1961).

M. Liebman, *The Russian Revolution: Origin, Phases and Meaning of the Bolshevik Victory* (London, 1970).

R. Service, *The Russian Revolution, 1900–1927* (London, 1986).

N. Sobelev (ed.), *History of the October Revolution*, 2nd edn (Moscow, 1966).

L. Trotsky, *History of the Russian Revolution* (London, 1933).

More specialized works on aspects of 1917

M. Ferro, *The Russian Revolution of February 1917* (London, 1972).

M. Ferro, *The Bolshevik Revolution: A Social History of the Russian Revolution* (London, 1980).

G. Gill, *Peasants and Government in the Russian Revolution* (London, 1979).

T. Hasegawa, *The February Revolution: Petrograd 1917* (Seattle, 1981).

J. Keep, *The Russian Revolution: A Study in Mass Mobilisation* (London, 1976).

D. Koenker, *Moscow Workers and the 1917 Revolution* (Princeton, 1981).

S. Melgunov, *The Bolshevik Seizure of Power* (Oxford, 1972).

R. Pethybridge, *The Spread of the Revolution 1917* (London 1972).

A. Rabinowitch, *The Bolsheviks Come to Power* (New York, 1976).

R. Service, *The Bolshevik Party in Revolution, 1917–1923: A Study in Organisational Change* (London, 1982).

S. Smith, *Red Petrograd: Revolution in the Factories, 1917–1918* (Cambridge, 1983).

R. G. Suny, *The Baku Commune, 1917–1918: Class and Nationality in the Russian Revolution* (Princeton, 1972).

A. Wildman, *The End of the Russian Imperial Army: The Old Army and the Soldiers' Revolt (March–April 1917)* (Princeton, 1980).

Works published since the first edition

E. Acton, *Rethinking the Russian Revolution* (London, 1990).

A. Ascher, *The Revolution of 1905. Russia in Disarray* (Stanford, 1988).

A. Ascher, *The Revolution of 1905. Authority Restored* (Stanford, 1992).

J. Bushnell, *Mutiny and Repression. Russian Soldiers in the Revolution of 1905–1906* (Indiana, 1987).

O. Crisp and L. Edmondson (eds), *Civil Rights in Imperial Russia* (Oxford, 1989).

O. Figes, *Peasant Russia, Civil War. The Volga Countryside in Revolution 1917–1921* (Oxford, 1989).

E. R. Frankel, J. Frankel and B. Knei-Paz (eds), *Revolution in Russia: Reassessments of 1917* (Cambridge, 1992).

D. H. Kaiser (ed.), *The Workers' Revolution in Russia, 1917. The View from Below* (Cambridge, 1987).

R. Pipes, *The Russian Revolution, 1899–1919* (London, 1992).

D. J. Raleigh, *Revolution on the Volga: 1917 in Saratov* (Ithaca, 1986).

D. Saunders, *Russia in the Age of Reaction and Reform, 1801–1881* (London, 1992).

R. Service, *Lenin: A Political Life*, vol. 2: *Worlds in Collision* (London, 1991).

See also:

The articles published in *European History Quarterly*, special issue: *Rewriting Russia 1917*, vol. 22, no. 4, October 1992.

The twice-yearly journal, *Revolutionary Russia*, which publishes the results of the most up-to-date research in this field.